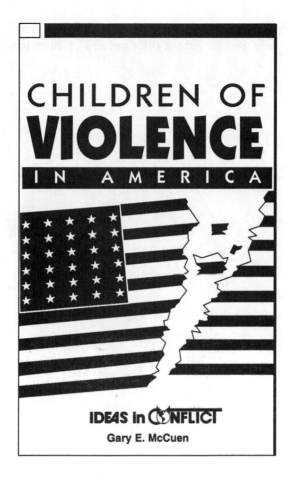

CHILDREN OF
VIOLENCE
IN AMERICA

IDEAS in CONFLICT

Gary E. McCuen

411 Mallalieu Drive
Hudson, Wisconsin 54016
Phone (715) 386-7113

Illustration and Photo Credits

Tony Auth 32; Steve Benson 45, 119; Chris Britt 28; David Catrow 59; Centers for Disease Control and Prevention 11, 17, 24; Bob Gorrell 40, 125; Joe Heller 99, 148; Mike Keefe 64; Jeff MacNelly 71; Gary Markstein 83, 159; Eleanor Mill 137; Mike Peters 143; Mike Ramirez 79, 88, 131; Bob Rogers 93; Steve Sack 50; Joe Sharpnack 152.

publications inc.

© 1995 by Gary E. McCuen Publications, Inc.
411 Mallalieu Drive, Hudson, Wisconsin 54016

(715) 386-7113

International Standard Book Number
ISBN 0-86596-095-X
Printed in the United States of America

CONTENTS

Ideas in Conflict

Chapter 1   YOUTH VIOLENCE IN AMERICA: AN OVERVIEW

Chapter 2   VIOLENCE IN SCHOOLS

Chapter 3   GANGS, GUNS, AND VIOLENCE

Chapter 4   PREVENTING YOUTH VIOLENCE

REASONING SKILL DEVELOPMENT

These activities may be used as individualized study guides for students in libraries and resource centers or as discussion catalysts in small group and classroom discussions.

IDEAS in CONFLICT

This series features ideas in conflict on political, social, and moral issues. It presents counterpoints, debates, opinions, commentary, and analysis for use in libraries and classrooms. Each title in the series uses one or more of the following basic elements:

Introductions *that present an issue overview giving historic background and/or a description of the controversy.*

Counterpoints *and debates carefully chosen from publications, books, and position papers on the political right and left to help librarians and teachers respond to requests that treatment of public issues be fair and balanced.*

Symposiums *and forums that go beyond debates that can polarize and oversimplify. These present commentary from across the political spectrum that reflect how complex issues attract many shades of opinion.*

A **global** *emphasis with foreign perspectives and surveys on various moral questions and political issues that will help readers to place subject matter in a less culture-bound and ethnocentric frame of reference. In an ever-shrinking and interdependent world, understanding and cooperation are essential. Many issues are global in nature and can be effectively dealt with only by common efforts and international understanding.*

Reasoning skill *study guides and discussion activities provide ready-made tools for helping with critical reading and evaluation of content. The guides and activities deal with one or more of the following:*

RECOGNIZING AUTHOR'S POINT OF VIEW

INTERPRETING EDITORIAL CARTOONS

VALUES IN CONFLICT

WHAT IS EDITORIAL BIAS?

WHAT IS SEX BIAS?

WHAT IS POLITICAL BIAS?

WHAT IS ETHNOCENTRIC BIAS?

WHAT IS RACE BIAS?

WHAT IS RELIGIOUS BIAS?

*From across **the political spectrum** varied sources are presented for research projects and classroom discussions. Diverse opinions in the series come from magazines, newspapers, syndicated columnists, books, political speeches, foreign nations, and position papers by corporations and nonprofit institutions.*

About the Editor

Gary E. McCuen is an editor and publisher of anthologies for public libraries and curriculum materials for schools. Over the past years his publications have specialized in social, moral and political conflict. They include books, pamphlets, cassettes, tabloids, filmstrips and simulation games, many of them designed from his curriculums during 11 years of teaching junior and senior high school social studies. At present he is the editor and publisher of the *Ideas in Conflict* series.

CHAPTER 1

YOUTH VIOLENCE IN AMERICA:
AN OVERVIEW

1
YOUTH VIOLENCE IN AMERICA: AN OVERVIEW

THE EPIDEMIC
OF YOUTH VIOLENCE

Select Committee on Youth, Violence and Families

The following article was excerpted from a fact sheet prepared for a joint hearing by the House Select Committee on Children, Youth, and Families and the Subcommittee on Children, Family, Drugs and Alcoholism of the Senate Committee on Labor and Human Resources.

Points to Consider:

1. How do children witness and participate in violence?

2. What statistics show that young people are disproportionate victims of violent crime?

3. What is the relationship between firearms and youth violence?

4. How much does youth violence cost America?

5. Why is the U.S. the most violent "civilized" nation in the world?

Excerpted from a joint Congressional hearing titled "Keeping Every Child Safe: Curbing the Epidemic of Violence" before the House Select Committee on Children, Youth, and Families and the Subcommittee on Children, Family, Drugs and Alcoholism of the Senate Committee on Labor and Human Resources, March 10, 1993.

YOUTH FACE INCREASINGLY HIGH RISK OF DEATH, INJURY

—In 1989, homicide was the third leading cause of death among children ages 5-14, and the second leading cause of death in the 15-24 age group. From 1979 to 1989, the firearm homicide rate for persons 15-19 increased 61.%. (Health United States [HUS], 1991; Fingerhut, et al., 1992)

—Between 1985 and 1989, the age-adjusted homicide rate increased 74% for African-American males ages 15-34, making it the leading cause of death for this group. In 1989, the age-adjusted homicide rate for African-American males ages 15-24 was almost nine times that for whites. (HUS, 1991)

—Male youth in the U.S. are more than five times as likely to be victims of homicide as youth in many other developed countries. (Select Committee on Children, Youth, and Families, 1990)

In a 1990 national survey, nearly 8% of all students in grades 9-12 (12.2% for males and 3.6% for females) reported that, during the 30 days preceding the survey, they had been in at least one physical fight that resulted in an injury requiring treatment by a doctor or nurse. (Centers for Disease Control [CDC], 1992)

YOUNG CHILDREN WITNESS, PARTICIPATE IN VIOLENCE

—In surveys of New Orleans, LA, and Washington, DC, inner-city children ages 6-10, over 90% had witnessed some type of violence. Thirty-seven percent had witnessed severe violence, almost 40% had seen dead bodies, and over 70% had witnessed weapons being used. Thirty to 40% of the New Orleans children and 15-20% of the Washington, DC, children said they worried about being safe. (Richters and Martinez, 1992; Osofsky, et al., 1992)

—Of 2,016 weapons brought to Virginia schools during the 1991-92 school year, 853 involved middle school students, compared with 748 which involved high school students. (Virginia Department of Education, 1993)

—Fifty-four percent of middle school and 56% of elementary school principals report more violent acts in their schools than 5 years ago. (*The Executive Educator*, 1993)

Gun-related deaths

Here's a breakdown of the 38,317 firearm deaths in the U.S. in 1991.

Homicide	17,746
Suicide	18,526
Accidents	1,441
Other/unknown	604

Source: Centers for Disease Control and Prevention

Reprinted with permission from **Star Tribune,** Minneapolis - St. Paul.

YOUTH DISPROPORTIONATE VICTIMS OF VIOLENT CRIME

–Children and youth ages 12 to 24 face the highest risk of non-fatal violent victimization of any segment of society. The assault rate alone was 44 times greater for youth ages 16 to 19 than for the elderly (79.2 per 1,000 persons age 16 to 19 compared with 1.8 per 1,000 persons 65 or older). (Rosenberg, 1992; Bureau of Justice Statistics [BJS], 1992)

–In 1991, the overall victimization rate for crimes of violence was nearly 16 times higher for those under age 25 than for persons age 65 or older. (BJS, 1993)

SCHOOLS INCREASINGLY DANGEROUS PLACE FOR CHILDREN, TEACHERS

–Each day, 100,000 children carry guns to school. In a national survey, 20% of all students in grade 9-12 reported that they had carried a weapon at least once during the preceding 30 days.

11

(Department of Justice [DOJ], 1993; CDC, 1991)

–Every hour, 900 teachers are threatened, nearly 40 teachers are physically attacked, and over 2,000 students are physically attacked on school grounds. (DOJ, 1993)

YOUTH COMMIT HIGH RATE OF VIOLENT CRIME

–In 1990, the United States experienced its highest juvenile violent crime arrest rate (430 per 100,000 juveniles), up 27% since 1980. During the 1980s, the white juvenile violent crime arrest rate increased 44%, compared with a 19% increase for African-American youth, and a 53% decrease for others. (Federal Bureau of Investigation [FBI], 1993)

–During the 1980s, youth between the ages of 12 and 24 committed more than 48,000 homicides, and during 1989, nearly half of about 4.2 million nonfatal violent crimes. Between 1965 and 1990, juvenile arrests for murder increased 332% (from 2.8 per 100,000 to 12.1 per 100,000). (Rosenberg, 1992; FBI, 1992)

URBAN YOUTH AT GREATER RISK OF VIOLENCE, BUT NONURBAN YOUTH ALSO AT RISK

–The 1989 firearm homicide rate in metropolitan counties for persons 15 to 19 years of age was nearly five times the rate in nonmetropolitan counties. The nonfirearm homicide rate for urban areas was 1.4 times the rate in nonmetropolitan counties. (Fingerhut, et al., 1992)

–In a survey of inner-city and middle-to-upper income youth, 42% of inner-city males reported that their lives had been threatened, compared with 18% of middle-to-upper income males. While 67% of inner-city adolescents knew someone who had been assaulted, so did 25% of youth in the middle-to-upper income group. (Gladstein, et al., 1992)

–Gangs were once a problem of primarily large urban areas; today gangs exist in cities with populations as small as 8,000. (Congressional Research Service, 1992)

FIREARMS EASILY OBTAINED, INVOLVED IN MOST DEADLY VIOLENCE

–Every day, 40 children are killed or injured by guns. (DOJ, 1993)

MOST VIOLENT COUNTRY

The United States, we are sorry to say, is the most violent "civilized" country in the world.   When you look at the international comparison figures among males 15 to 24 years of age, the conclusions are astounding.   For instance, in France, for that age group, 2 homicides per 100,000; Australia, 3 per 100,000; Norway, 4 per 100,000; Scotland, 5 per 100,000; United States, 22 per 100,000. Scotland is second at 5 homicides per 100,000 persons, so the United States is 4 1/2 times more violent than the country in second place.

The breakdown within the figures for African Americans just blows your mind. It is over 85 homicides per 100,000 persons for young people in that age group. A tragic loss of life, 85 homicides per 100,000 persons. According to the Department of Justice and the (Centers for Disease Control) CDC, the following facts exist: Young males aged 15 to 34 are the most likely to die as a result of homicide. In this country, while all young males are at risk, African-American males aged 15 to 24 are at highest risk. Tragically, these men, are in fact, at a higher risk to die of a violent homicide than those who served during the war in the Persian Gulf.

Non-homicidal violent crime, such as aggravated assault, simple assault, and rape, is most likely to be committed by people under 25. These people are also the most likely victims of these crimes.

Firearms are the weapons of choice for most violent acts. From 1984 through 1987, 80.1 percent of all youth homicides were committed with firearms. Among young black males, according to CDC, there has been a dramatic 54 percent increase in homicides, with 99 percent of the increase due to firearms. A serious strategy on the reduction of youth violence must address firearms on the streets.

Excerpted from testimony by Senator John Glen of Ohio, March 31, 1992.

–In 1990, nearly three of every four youthful murderers used a firearm. A 79% increase in the number of juveniles committing murder with guns was reported over the past decade. (FBI, 1993; FBI 1992)

–A Baltimore, MD, hospital experienced a sharp increase in the admission of pediatric gunshot victims, from five in 1986 to 26 in 1991. Twenty-two victims were admitted in the first half of 1992. (Nicholas, 1992)

–In a survey of Seattle, WA, high school students, 34% of the students reported easy access to handguns and 6.4% reported owning a handgun. (Callahan and Rivara, 1992)

VIOLENCE COSTS SOCIETY BILLIONS

–Taxpayers spend $1.7 billion annually to house incarcerated youth, at an average annual per-resident cost of $29,600. (U.S. General Accounting Office, 1992)

–Nationally, total health care costs because of criminal violence were estimated to be more than $3.5 billion, with $1.5 billion resulting from firearms. (Billings and Teicholz, 1991)

–In a study based on 1985 data, interpersonal violence was estimated to account for 14% of all injury deaths at an estimated annual cost of $10.9 billion. (Rice, et al., 1989)

–Washington, DC, hospitals spend at least $20.4 million a year treating victims of shootings, stabbings, and other crimes. If health care expenses after leaving the hospital are included, the costs would increase to $40 million. (Billings and Teicholz, 1991)

2 YOUTH VIOLENCE IN AMERICA: AN OVERVIEW

MINORITY YOUTH VIOLENCE

John Hagan

John Hagan is a professor of Sociology and Law in the School of Law at the University of Toronto in Ontario, Canada.

Points to Consider:

1. How is the imprisonment rate for young black males described?

2. What are the racial patterns of crime in America?

3. Who is Alex Kotlowitz? Douglas Massey?

4. Explain the relationship between racial discrimination and crime.

Excerpted from Congressional testimony before the Subcommittee on Human Resources of the House Committee on Ways and Means, December 7, 1993.

*Minority youth are disproportionately both the vic-
tims and perpetrators of crime in the United States.*

America's juvenile and criminal justice systems are prominent
institutions in the adolescent and early adult lives of the inner city
poor. When impoverished minority youth are not a part of families or attending schools, they are especially likely to be swept
into the juvenile and criminal justice systems. The imprisonment
rate for young black males is more than four times that for whites,
and it is estimated that three of every four black male school drop-
outs come under supervision of the criminal justice system by the
time they reach their early 30's. As justice system contacts and
expenditures have increased in recent years, rates of violent crime
have not diminished. For example, homicide is now a leading
cause of death for young black males, and this death rate soared
during the "War on Drugs" of the mid to late 1980s.

VICTIMS, PERPETRATORS AND POVERTY

Minority youth are disproportionately both the victims and perpetrators of crime in the United States, and crime victimization is
a pervasive part of black community life more generally. For
example, the U.S. Department of Justice's annual National Crime
Survey, a nationwide residential survey of the general public and
their experiences as victims of crime, shows that blacks experience rates of robbery victimization that are more than 150 percent
higher than those for whites. For much of the last half century,
rates of black homicide deaths have ranged from six to seven
times those for whites. These patterns reflect the danger, anger,
risks and strains of crime in poor urban areas. In his poignant
book *There Are No Children Here*, about the early teenage years
of the brothers Pharaoh and Lafayette Rivers, Alex Kotlowitz
reports the younger brother as confiding, "I worry about dying,
dying at a young age, while you're little." Surveys indicate that
parents in these neighborhoods share these fears.

For many youths, victimization is a consequence of the risk of
living in a highly criminal environment; for others, it is a consequence of direct participation in the criminal activities that prevail
in this environment. Victimization often leads to offending, and
much crime in minority neighborhoods is a product of retaliation
and revenge-seeking acts that are a common part of gang and
peer group associations. Turf battles are common within and
between racial and ethnic enclaves and ghettos. The line

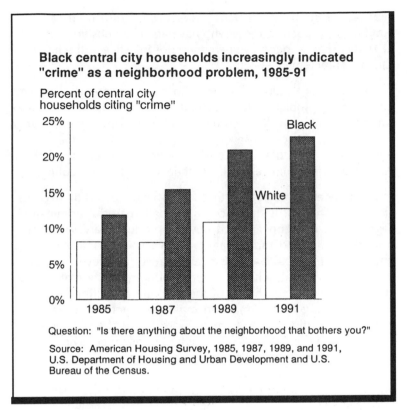

Black central city households increasingly indicated "crime" as a neighborhood problem, 1985-91

Percent of central city households citing "crime"

Question: "Is there anything about the neighborhood that bothers you?"

Source: American Housing Survey, 1985, 1987, 1989, and 1991, U.S. Department of Housing and Urban Development and U.S. Bureau of the Census.

Centers for Disease Control and Prevention.

between victimization and offending in such episodes often is unclear; the acts involved can be partly a reflection and partly a cause of a pattern of "diffuse aggression."

HIGH CRIME AREAS

Even living in proximity to high-crime areas increases the risk of crime victimization, so that the middle-class and near-poor members of minority communities suffer as much or more crime victimization as impoverished members of these communities. Public opinion surveys indicate that many middle-class black Americans believe that the police and courts fail to protect them from the growing problems of crime, and at the same time mistreat them in their encounters with justice officials. These perceptions have been reinforced by the Rodney King beating and similar encounters, but middle-class black Americans have long complained of such harassment. Research confirms that black Americans, especially those who have achieved positions of higher status, share a pervasive perception of injustice at the hands of the law enforcement system.

Young black American males who experience education and employment problems are at exceptionally high risk of arrest and imprisonment as well as criminal victimization. One in every three arrests and one in every two incarcerations in the United States involves a black American. Three in every four black American prison inmates have less than 12 years of schooling.

Scholarly efforts to explain these facts have focused on two possibilities. The first is that race-linked patterns of discrimination, segregation, and concentrated poverty produce pervasive family and community disadvantages, as well as educational and employment difficulties, that in turn cause high levels of delinquent and criminal behavior among young minority males. The second is that, at the hands of the juvenile and criminal justice systems, young black American males are victims of prejudice and discrimination in the form of more frequent arrest, prosecution, and punishment for delinquent and criminal behavior. There is evidence for both of these explanations, and an awareness of their combined validity adds an important element of suspicion and distrust to minority citizens interactions with the justice system.

MINORITY SETTINGS

Increasing attention is focused on the ways in which these problems have become concentrated in distressed minority settings. Sociologists such as William Julius Wilson and Robert Sampson emphasize that violent street crime and victimization are increasingly concentrated in distressed minority neighborhoods because of the concentration of poverty and joblessness in these settings. The demographer Douglas Massey, in his study *American Apartheid*, argues that racial segregation was a further factor responsible for the transformation of many black communities beginning in the 1970s. This work shows how a pernicious interaction involving the loss of jobs and high levels of segregation created a population often identified as an "underclass," transforming low-income communities into places where welfare-dependent, female-headed families are the norm. When this occurs, patterns of formal and informal community control are

18

undermined, in turn producing high rates of crime and related problems. The social capital of these communities is depleted and no longer can be effectively mobilized to contain the strains and pressures that lead to crime.

CONCENTRATED POVERTY

Community studies are especially persuasive in describing the ways in which concentrated poverty affects crime rates in minority neighborhoods. Recent ethnographics, such as Elijah Anderson's *Streetwise*, emphasize the growth of the underground drug economy focused around gangs and guns, which substitutes and competes with the legitimate labor market. Anderson points out that for many young minority males the drug economy is an illicit employment agency super-imposed on existing gang networks. Youth who come of age in gangs and who have never experienced sustained legal employment find a place in the illicit economy made up of the selling of drugs on street corners and in drug houses. The violence that accompanies these activities is reflected in racial differences in homicide rates reported above. However, it is extremely important to recognize that these racial differences only persist in contexts of concentrated poverty. Epidemiological studies indicate that at higher socioeconomic levels, blacks and whites experience similarly low rates of homicide; only in areas with high concentrations of poor families do black Americans experience higher levels of homicide victimization.

CONCLUSIONS

High levels of crime among minority youth are causally associated with the concentration of poverty in urban neighborhoods. Patterns of ethnic, especially racial, segregation have created conditions in which economic downturns and concentrated poverty have torn the social fabric of low-income minority communities.

Social disruption has aggravated stereotypes of these distressed community settings and has led to overpolicing and other kinds of punitive treatment that generate diffuse and pervasive feelings of injustice, hostility, and aggression. Hostility is itself disorganizing and disruptive in ways that make crime and violence common.

3   YOUTH VIOLENCE IN AMERICA: AN OVERVIEW

TEEN MALE HOMICIDE RATE SOARS

Centers for Disease Control and Prevention

The following report was taken from the Mortality and Morbidity Weekly Report (MMWR) *series prepared by the Centers for Disease Control and Prevention and is available on a paid subscription basis from the Superintendent of Documents, U.S. Government Printing Office, Washington DC 20402; telephone (202) 783-3238.*

Points to Consider:

1. Explain the relationship of homicide victims and the death rate.

2. How much has the homicide rate increased?

3. What age groups have experienced the fastest growth in homicide rates?

4. Describe the factors that may have led to the rapid increase in homicide.

5. What strategies might be used to prevent homicides?

"Homicides Among 15-19 Year Old Males-United States, 1963-1991," **Morbidity and Mortality Weekly Report (MMWR)**, Vol. 43, No. 40, October 14, 1994.

The homicide rate for persons aged 15–34 years increased 50% during this period.

In 1991, nearly half (13,122 [49%]) of the 26,513 homicide victims in the United States were males aged 15–34 years. In addition, among males in this age group, homicide accounted for 18% of all deaths and was the second leading cause of death (Table 1). During 1963–1991, the pattern of homicide rates changed substantially; the change was greatest for males aged 15–19 years, for whom rates increased substantially. This report summarizes these trends and presents strategies for violence prevention and intervention.

Mortality data were obtained from CDC's National Center for Health Statistics; population estimates were projected from census data. Arrest rates were calculated using data from the U.S. Department of Justice.

From 1985 to 1991, the annual crude homicide rate for the United States increased 25% (from 8.4 to 10.5 per 100,000 persons). The homicide rate for persons aged 15–34 years increased 50% during this period (from 13.4 to 20.1 per 100,000), accounting for most of the overall increase. Rates increased for both sexes and all 5-year age groups within the 15–34-year age group. For persons in other age groups, rates were relatively stable from 1985 to 1991: for persons aged ≤14 years, 1.9 and 2.4, respectively; for persons aged 35–64 years, 8.8 and 9.1, respectively; and for persons aged ≥65 years, 4.3 and 4.1, respectively.

Table 1. Leading causes of death for males aged 15–34 years United States, 1991		
Cause	No.	(%)
Unintentional injury	23,108	(32)
Homicide	13,122	(18)
Suicide	9,434	(13)
HIV infection	8,661	(12)
Cancer	3,699	(5)
Other	13,234	(19)
Total	71,258	(100)

From 1963 through 1985, annual homicide rates for 15–19-year-old males were one third to one half the rates for the next three higher 5-year age groups (Figure 1). However, during 1985–1991, annual rates for males aged 15–19 years increased 154% (from 13.0 to 33.0), surpassing the rates for 25–29- and 30–34-year-old males, even though those rates increased 32% (from 24.4 to 32.3) and 16% (from 22.1 to 25.7), respectively. The homicide rate for 20–24-year-old males increased 76% (from 23.4 to 41.2) from 1985 through 1991.

During 1985–1991, age-specific arrest rates for murder and non-negligent manslaughter increased 127% for males aged 15–19 years, 43% for males aged 20–24 years, and declined 1% and 13% for males aged 25–29 and 30–34 years, respectively. In 1991, 15–19-year-old males were more likely to be arrested for murder than males in any other age group.

Above information reported by: *Div. of Violence Prevention, National Center for Injury Prevention and Control, CDC.*

Editorial Note: The increase in the annual homicide rate for 15–19-year-old males during 1985–1991 was a dramatic change from the pattern during 1963–1984. Although the immediate and specific causes of this problem are unclear, the increase in the occurrence of homicide may be the result of the recruitment of juveniles into drug markets, the use of guns in these markets, and the consequent diffusion of guns to other young persons in the community, resulting, in turn, in more frequent use of the guns for settling disputes. Among 15–19-year-old males, firearm-related homicides accounted for 88% of all homicides in 1991 and 97% of the increase in the rate from 1985 through 1991. Factors underlying the immediate precursors may include poverty, inade-

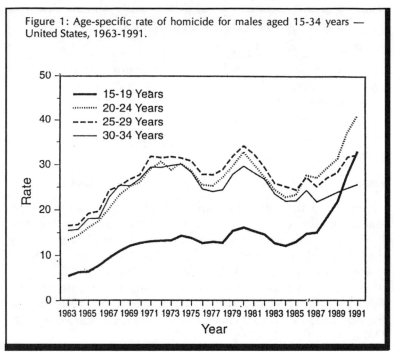

Figure 1: Age-specific rate of homicide for males aged 15-34 years — United States, 1963-1991.

Centers for Disease Control and Prevention.

quate educational and economic opportunities, social and family instability, and frequent personal exposure to violence as an acceptable or preferred method of resolving disagreements.

Although the most effective strategies to prevent youth violence have not been determined, efforts to prevent this problem should employ established principles of health promotion and should emphasize the use of multiple complementary interventions. These interventions include

Strengthening the science base for prevention efforts. Strategies and methods to prevent violence in youth should be rigorously assessed:

• *Establishing primary-prevention programs.* Primary-prevention aims to prevent the occurrence of violence rather than focusing on known perpetrators and victims after the occurrence of violence. This strategy addresses all forms of violence (e.g., spouse abuse, child abuse, and violence among youth) and could affect both potential perpetrators and victims.

24

- *Targeting youths of all ages.* Violence-reduction efforts should address the needs of infants, children, and older youths. Measures that have been successful in reducing violent behavior and its precursors in these age groups should be considered when developing new programs.

- *Involving adults (e.g., parents and other role models).* They influence violence-related attitudes and behaviors of youth and should be provided the appropriate knowledge and skills to function as role models.

- *Presenting messages in multiple settings.* Lessons in one setting (e.g., a school) should be reinforced in other settings in which children and youth congregate, including homes, churches, recreational settings, and clinics.

- *Addressing societal and personal factors.* Societal factors (e.g., poverty, unemployment, under-education, and social acceptance of violence) should be addressed simultaneously with efforts to affect personal behavior change through activities such as home visitation, school-based training, or mentoring.

4   YOUTH VIOLENCE IN AMERICA: AN OVERVIEW

YOUTH GANGS

U.S. Department of Justice

The following article was excerpted from a publication on youth violence by the Office of Juvenile Justice and Delinquency Prevention in the United States Department of Justice.

Points to Consider:

1. How extensively are gangs organized in the U.S.?

2. Explain the nature and extent of gang criminal activity.

3. What strategies can be used to deal with gang activities?

4. Describe the most effective strategy to deal with gangs in our cities.

Office of Juvenile Justice and Delinquency Prevention in the United States Department of Justice, "Comprehensive Strategy for Serious, Violent, and Chronic Juvenile Offenders," December 1993.

Police officials in 35 emerging and chronic gang-problem cities estimated the presence of 1,439 gangs and 120,636 gang members.

In the late 1970s, Walter Miller conducted the first nationwide study of youth gangs (Miller, 1975, 1982). The study found youth gang problems in half of the Nation's large (more than 1 million population) metropolitan areas. The 10 largest gang-problem cities contained about half the gangs. Miller estimated that 300 U.S. cities and towns contained about 2,300 youth gangs, with nearly 100,000 members. About 3,400 youth gang-related killings were reported for about 60 cities during a 13-year period ending in 1980. Miller's major conclusions were:

• By 1980 there were more gang members in the United States than at any time in the past.

• Youth gangs were active in more cities than at any other time.

• Gang crime was more lethal than at any time in history; more people were shot, stabbed, and beaten to death in gang-related incidents than during any previous decade.

• Members of gangs and other groups were more heavily armed than at any time in the past. Such groups have always used weapons, but the prevalence and sophistication of firearms used in the 1970s was unprecedented.

• The amount of property destruction by gangs through vandalism and arson of schools, residential and commercial buildings, and automobiles was more extensive and costly than in any previous decade.

Research designed to estimate the numbers and characteristics of youth gangs in the United States has not been conducted since Miller's study. However, Spergel and his colleagues (Spergel et al., 1990, 1991) completed a nationwide assessment of promising approaches to preventing and intervening in youth gangs. In the course of this research Spergel made the following observations:

• The scope and seriousness of the youth gang problem nationally is not clearly or reliably known. Police officials in 35 emerging and chronic gang-problem cities estimated the presence of 1,439 gangs and 120,636 gang members.

• Based on law enforcement and media reports, criminal youth

Cartoon by Chris Britt. Reprinted with permission of **Coply News Service.**

gangs or gang members are to be found in nearly all 50 States.

• Evidence exists of a general increase in gang-related violence in several cities, particularly on the west coast.

• Gang members with arrest records are responsible for a disproportionate amount of violent crime. At the same time, the proportion of total violent crime committed by gang members is very low.

• Gang violence is concentrated in certain categories of violent crime, such as homicide and aggravated assault, and is concentrated in certain neighborhoods.

• Historically, youth gangs have rarely engaged in drug dealing, especially hard drugs. Recently, some youth gangs have become involved in street sale of drugs.

• The age range of gang members has expanded in recent decades. Members remain in gangs longer. Extreme gang violence is concentrated in the older teen and young adult range. The average age of the arrested gang offender is 17 to 18. The average age of the gang homicide offender is 19 to 20.

• Several observers suggest a close relationship between youth

GANG VIOLENCE

Little Rock, with a population of 177,000, is experiencing a big-city epidemic of gangs, guns, crack and murder. It had a record 61 murders in 1992, up from 52 in 1991 and an average of 37 over the five years before that. For the past two years, Little Rock's murder rate in relation to population has equaled that of New York or Los Angeles.

Erik Eckholm, "Little Rock Is Experiencing Epidemic of Gang Problems," **New York Times**, February, 1993.

gangs and organized crime. Youth gang structures, or cliques within gangs, are sometimes seen as sub-units of organized crime and are employed for purposes of drug distribution, auto theft, extortion, and burglary.

Spergel's research revealed that five basic strategies have evolved in dealing with young gangs: (1) suppression, (2) social intervention, (3) social opportunities, (4) community mobilization, and (5) organizational development or change. Community mobilization, including improved communication and joint policy and program development among justice, community-based, and grassroots organizations, appears to be an effective primary strategy in both emerging gang-problem cities and in those with chronic gang problems.

5   YOUTH VIOLENCE IN AMERICA: AN OVERVIEW

STREET GANGS IN CHICAGO

Carolyn Rebecca Block and Richard Block

Carolyn Rebecca Block is senior analyst at the Statistical Analysis Center, Illinois Criminal Justice Information Authority. Richard Block is professor of sociology at Loyola University in Chicago. The following statement is excerpted from an article they wrote for the National Institute of Justice.

Points to Consider:

1. How extensive and varied are street gang - motivated offenses?

2. Compare the nature of the four largest gangs in Chicago.

3. Identify the specific kinds of gang-related criminal activities.

4. Explain the difference between "instrumental violence" and "expressive violence."

5. What are the public policy implications of gangs and gang-related violence?

Carolyn Rebecca Block and Richard Block, "Street Gang Crime in Chicago," **Research in Brief**, National Institute of Justice, December 1993.

More than 40 major street gangs are active in the city of Chicago.

Street gang activity–legal and illegal, violent and nonviolent, lethal and nonlethal–occurs disproportionately among neighborhoods and population groups. Types of incidents tend to cluster and increase in bursts in specific neighborhoods and among specific gangs.

Neighborhoods often differ sharply in the predominant type of street gang-motivated incidents they experience. For example, one city neighborhood may be unaffected by street gang activity, while another close by may be a marketplace for a street gang's drug operation, and yet a third may be plagued by frequent and lethal turf battles.

In addition, the chief criminal activities of one street gang often differ from those of another. For example, one outbreak of lethal street gang violence may be characterized by escalating retribution and revenge, while another may be associated with expansion of a drug business into new territory. Consequently, street gangs and the crimes in which they engage cannot be viewed as monolithic in nature.

This *Research in Brief* describes these and other patterns of street gang-related violence in a major U.S. city–Chicago. All available information, including Chicago police records of illegal street gang-motivated activity–from vandalism to drug offenses to violent offenses (both lethal and nonlethal)–was examined across time, neighborhood, and street gang affiliation. Individual, gang-level, and neighborhood-level characteristics were also analyzed to determine the relationships among these three factors. The results of the analysis give one of the most complete pictures of street gang crime available today.

DATA ON STREET GANG-MOTIVATED OFFENSES

This data set included information on 17,085 criminal offenses that occurred from 1987 to 1990 that were classified by the police as street gang-related. These offenses were categorized as follows:

• 288 homicides.

• 8,828 nonlethal violent offenses (aggravated and simple assault and battery).

31

"I SEE WHERE WE'RE DOING A LITTLE 'NATION-BUILDING' IN SOMALIA..."

• 5,888 drug offenses (violations related to possession or sale of hard or soft drugs).

• 2,081 other offenses (includes more than 100 specific crimes ranging from liquor law violations to intimidation, mob action, vandalism, robbery, and weapons law violations).

STREET GANGS IN THE CITY

More than 40 major street gangs are active in the city of Chicago. Researchers in this study concentrated on the four largest and most criminally active street gangs, each of which was responsible for at least 1,000 police-recorded criminal incidents from 1987 to 1990:

• *Black Gangster Disciples Nation (BGDN).* Descended from the Woodlawn Disciples, BGDN is strongest on Chicago's South Side. The gang is known for its turf wars with the Blackstone Rangers in the late 1960s and early 1970s and the Black Disciples in 1991.

• *Latin Disciples.* A racially and ethnically mixed street gang allied with BGDN, the Latin Disciples operate mainly in the integrated Northwest Side neighborhoods of Humboldt Park and Logan Square.

• **Latin Kings.** The oldest (over 25 years) and largest Latino street gang in Chicago, the Latin Kings operate throughout the city in Latino and racially and ethnically mixed neighborhoods. The gang is particularly active in the growing Mexican neighborhoods on the Southwest Side.

• **Vice Lords.** One of the oldest street gangs in Chicago, the Vice Lords date from the 1950s. The gang operates throughout the city, but is strongest in the very poor West Side neighborhoods that have never recovered from the destruction that followed the death of Dr. Martin Luther King in 1968.

Members of the BGDN and the Vice Lords are almost all black men, while the Latin Disciples and Latin Kings are predominantly Latino men. Rough police department estimates indicate that the 19,000 members of these four gangs constitute about half of all Chicago street gang members. In the mid-1980s BGDN and the Latin Disciples formed the Folk alliance. Soon after the Latin Kings and the Vice Lords formed the People alliance. Both "super alliances" of street gangs appeared following an increase of street gang-related homicide.

CRIMINAL ACTIVITIES OF STREET GANGS

From 1987 to 1990, the four largest street gangs were also the most criminally active. They accounted for 69 percent of all street gang-motivated crimes and 56 percent of all street gang-motivated homicides in which the street gang affiliation of the offender was known. Of the 17,085 street gang-motivated offenses recorded during this period, BGDN was responsible for 4,843 offenses; the Vice Lords for 3,116; the Latin Kings for 2,868; and the Latin Disciples for 1,011.

However, taken as a whole, street gangs other than the top four were responsible for more police-recorded offenses (5,207 from 1987 to 1990 than any one of the top four. Many of these smaller street gangs were relatively new, predominantly Latino, and fighting among themselves over limited turfs.

Drug offenses. The four major street gangs varied sharply in the degree to which drug crimes dominated their illegal activity. For example, of the 2,868 incidents committed by the Latin Kings from 1987 through 1990, only 19 percent were drug offenses, compared to 56 percent of the 3,116 incidents attributed to the Vice Lords. More incidents of cocaine possession (the most com-

33

mon drug offense) were attributed to the Vice Lords or to the Black Gangster Disciples Nation than to all other street gangs combined. The Vice Lords were also active in heroin possession offenses, with twice as many incidents attributed to them as to all other street gangs combined.

The reintroduction of heroin to Chicago by the Vice Lords and Black Gangster Disciples Nation was particularly disturbing to police and community workers. From 1987 to 1990, the number of incidents of possession of white heroin rapidly escalated from 11 to 165, while possession of brown heroin declined from 77 to 64, probably reflecting the reentry of Asian heroin into the Chicago market. Meanwhile, the number of incidents of hard drug possession involving the Latin Kings, Latin Disciples, and other street gangs remained low.

HIGHLIGHTS OF MAJOR FINDINGS

This study painted a more complete picture of the reality of street gang crime than is usually the case in studies of gangs. By analyzing police records of lethal and nonlethal street gang-motivated crimes, examining temporal and spatial patterns of those crimes, and describing the criminal activities of Chicago's four largest street gangs, researchers sought to uncover typical patterns of street gang life.

The patterns of street gang activity can be summarized as follows:

• Chicago's largest street gangs can be identified with most of the city's street gang crime. These four street gangs (representing about 10 percent of all street gangs and 51 percent of the estimated numbers of all street gang members) accounted for 69 percent of police-recorded street gang-motivated criminal incidents and 55 percent of all street gang-motivated homicides from 1987 to 1990.

• Street gangs varied in the types of activities in which they were engaged. Some specialized in incidents of *expressive violence* while others focused on *instrumental violence*. For example, the Vice Lords and BGDN were much more involved in acts of *instrumental violence* (such as possession or sale of drugs), while the Latin Disciples, Latin Kings, and smaller gangs specialized in acts of *expressive violence* (such as turf defense). Most of the criminal activity in smaller street gangs centered on turf defense. The most lethal street gang hot spot areas are along disputed boundaries between small street gangs.

• Types of street gang crime clustered in specific neighborhoods. Street gangs specializing in *instrumental violence* were strongest in disrupted and declining neighborhoods. Street gangs specializing in *expressive violence* were strongest and most violent in relatively prosperous neighborhoods with expanding populations.

• The rate of street gang-motivated crime in the two most dangerous Chicago communities was 76 times that of the two safest. However, every community area in Chicago had at least one street gang-motivated criminal incident between 1987 and 1990.

• Most of the lethal gang-related crimes occurred in neighborhoods where street gang activity centered on turf battles, not in neighborhoods where street gang activity focused on drug offenses. Of 288 street gang-motivated homicides from 1987 to 1990, only 8 also involved drug use or a drug-related motive.

• A gun was the lethal weapon in almost all Chicago street gang-motivated homicides from 1987 to 1990. Incidents involving a high-caliber, automatic, or semi-automatic weapon accounted for most of the increase in homicides over this period.

• Many community areas with high levels of lethal and non-lethal street gang-motivated personal violence and homicide had relatively low levels of other forms of homicide. Although hot spot areas of street gang-motivated drug offenses were usually low in street gang homicide, some were high in other kinds of homicide.

35

POLICY IMPLICATIONS

As this report shows, street gang violence has been a continuing problem in Chicago since the late 1960s. The years 1990, 1991, and 1992 broke records for street gang violence, and the number of incidents continued to grow in 1993.

Intervention programs whose aim is to reduce nonlethal street gang violence will probably also reduce lethal violence. To be effective, however, these intervention programs must be built on a foundation of current information about the types of street gangs and street gang activity in each specific neighborhood.

As shown by this research, street gang-motivated crime is not random. In Chicago it occurred in specific neighborhoods and was concentrated in limited time periods. Some street gangs spent much of their time defending or expanding their turf while others were actively involved in the business of illegal drugs. Programs to reduce street gang-motivated violence must recognize these differences. For example, a program to reduce gang involvement in drugs in a community in which gang members are most concerned with defense of turf has little chance of success.

Furthermore, because the predominant type of street gang activity in a neighborhood may change from year to year or month to month, and because the level of street gang-motivated violence tends to occur in spurts, effective intervention strategies must be built on continuously updated information.

Another focus of control over gang violence should be on weapons. The death weapon in almost all gang-motivated homicides in Chicago was a gun, and much of the increase in gang-motivated homicides from 1987 to 1990 was an increase in killings with large-caliber, automatic, or semi-automatic weapons. Therefore, reducing the availability of these most dangerous weapons may also reduce the risk of death in street gang-plagued communities.

Street gang membership, street gang-related violence, and other illegal street gang activity must be understood in light of both long-term or chronic social patterns, and current or acute conditions. Street gang patterns and trends reflect not only chronic problems, such as racial and class discrimination, but also acute, often rapidly changing problems stemming from the existing economic situation, weapon availability, drug markets, and the spa-

36

tial arrangement of street gang territories across a city.

Obviously, the chronic problem of street gang violence cannot be solved with a quick fix; the ultimate solution rests on a coordinated criminal justice response, changes in educational opportunities, racial and ethnic attitudes, and job structure. On the other hand, while waiting for these long-term strategies to take effect, lives can be saved and serious injury prevented by targeting the causes of short-term or acute escalations in violence levels.

6   YOUTH VIOLENCE IN AMERICA: AN OVERVIEW

SUICIDE AND GUN VIOLENCE

Josh Sugarmann
Kristen Rand

The following article was excerpted from "CEASE FIRE: A Comprehensive Strategy to Reduce Firearms Violence." It was written by Josh Sugarmann and Kristen Rand and published by the Violence Policy Center, 1300 N St. N.W., Washington, DC 20005, (202) 783-4071.

Points to Consider:

1. What has happened to the suicide rate in the recent past?

2. Explain the relationship between firearms, murder rates and suicide rates.

3. Compare the suicide rates between men and women.

4. Why do both proponents and opponents of gun control ignore the issue of suicide?

5. Why do suicide victims fail to arouse the level of sympathy reserved for other victims of firearms violence?

Josh Sugarmann and Kristen Rand. "Cease Fire: A Comprehensive Strategy to Reduce Firearms Violence." Violence Policy Center, ©1994 1300 N St. NW, Washington, DC 20005. Reprinted with permission.

If crime has become inextricably linked with the gun control debate, suicide has remained strangely outside its mainstream.

The increase in America's suicide rate has not been uniform but has fallen disproportionately to its youth and young adults. From 1961 to 1981 the suicide rate for Americans age 15 to 24 jumped 150 percent–from 5.1 per 100,000 in 1961 to 12.8 per 100,000 in 1981. Suicide has become the third leading cause of death for Americans in the 15-24 bracket (behind auto accidents and homicide).

Because teen suicide is often impulsive, firearms–which lend themselves well to spontaneity–pose a special hazard.

In light of the "apparently impulsive nature of teen suicide," authors Arthur Kellermann, Roberta Lee, James Mercy and Joyce Banton write, in their 1991 article "The Epidemiologic Basis for the Prevention of Firearm Injuries," that "the recent rise in the number of adolescents attempting suicide with firearms is particularly concerning, as guns provide little chance for salvage or rescue."

With the increased marketing of firearms–specifically handguns–to women for self defense, female patterns of suicide have also changed. Previously, a general rule of thumb was that women attempted to kill themselves two to three times more often than men. Men, however, succeeded three times more often than women, the reason being that women traditionally used pills or other less lethal means; men used guns. In 1970 poisoning was the suicide method most commonly used by women. This means has decreased in inverse proportion to handgun use. Now, like men, women most often kill themselves with firearms...

THE IGNORED GUN DEATHS: SUICIDE

For all our fear and fascination with guns and murder, the fact remains that most gun deaths in America are not a result of murder, but suicide. Over the past 20 years both sides in the gun control debate have characterized firearms violence as a crime issue. While pro-gun factions demand we "get tough" with criminals, gun control advocates devise schemes to "keep handguns out of the wrong hands." If crime has become inextricably linked with the gun control debate, suicide has remained strangely outside its mainstream. This is because suicide does not fit easily

Cartoon by Bob Gorrell. Reprinted with permission of **Coply News Service.**

into either side's schematics. Hence, it has been treated as something of an embarrassment and for the most part ignored.

Those with pro-gun sympathies tend to brush the subject aside with the observation that suicide victims would find a way to kill themselves "no matter what."

On the pro-control side, although gun suicides represent the "silent majority" of firearms victims, it is an issue many are loathe to deal with. First, focusing on suicide contradicts the perception that firearms violence results from guns finding their way into criminal hands. Any effort to address suicide requires abandonment of the "gun control" as "crime control" argument and the controversial acknowledgment that the problem lies not only with guns in criminal hands–but also in the law-abiding. Compounding this is the fact that the general public views victims of suicide far less sympathetically than firearms murder or accident victims, agreeing for the most part that they will kill themselves "no matter what."…

Surprisingly, even though suicide is the most common method of firearms death in America, good data is limited. *The Statistical Abstract of the United States* lists the annual total of firearm suicides as discerned from death certificates. Yet, because death certificates and medical examiners' reports in the United States are not standardized and not all specify the type of firearms used, the actual number of handgun suicides is unknown and can only be estimated...

SYMPATHY

Suicide victims do fail to arouse the level of sympathy reserved for other victims of firearms violence, but to argue that they will kill themselves "no matter what" holds true for only a small percentage. Psychologists note a consistent pattern for most suicides. The victim is depressed, often under the influence of drugs or alcohol. An event occurs that gives the victim for a brief period the will to die. The person will then use whatever means is at hand to attempt to kill himself. For the vast majority of those who attempt suicide–an estimated 90 percent–the success of the attempt depends primarily on the lethality of the means employed. Most suicide means either allow time for a change of heart–or are of limited lethality. With medical intervention, most who attempt suicide can be saved.

For example, self-inflicted cutting wounds account for 15 percent of all non-fatal suicide attempts in the U.S., but only 1 percent of all successful suicides. The ingestion of poisons or drugs accounts for 70 percent of all nonfatal suicide attempts, but less than 12 percent of all suicides. Conversely, nonfatal, self-inflicted gunshot wounds are rare–yet three-fifths of all U.S. suicides involve firearms. One study reported that 92 percent of suicide attempts by firearms were successful. Those who use firearms to kill themselves aren't by definition more suicidal than those who use other means and survive: they most likely just had the ill fortune of having a firearm nearby.

The few who survive firearms suicide attempts are often left disabled or disfigured. Writing in the February 1984 *American Journal of Public Health*, Dr. Joseph Westermeyer noted, "Over the past score of years, I have encountered many patients

41

who–after surviving gunshot wounds, usually to the head or abdomen–were disabled often for life with various degrees of disfigurement, difficulty eating and speaking, blindness, deafness, paralysis and/or dementia."

7

YOUTH VIOLENCE IN AMERICA: AN OVERVIEW

VIOLENT HOMES AND VIOLENT CHILDREN

Adele Harrell

Adele Harrell is a senior research analyst for the Urban Institute in Washington, DC.

Points to Consider:

1. How extensive is the problem of family violence directed at women and children?

2. What kinds of threats do women and children face?

3. Explain the effects of family violence on children.

4. Discuss ways that society can prevent family violence.

5. Define the term "cycle of violence."

Excerpted from testimony by Adele Harrell before the Senate Committee on Governmental Affairs, March 31, 1992.

With regard to delinquency, for example, over half the families reported for child abuse in one New York county later had at least one child appear in juvenile court.

One of the truly shocking facts about the problem of violence in this country, one that most of us would prefer to ignore, is the amount that occurs within the family—most of it directed at women and children. A few statistics illustrate the magnitude of the problem:

• Each year, more women are abused by their husbands or boyfriends than are injured in car accidents, muggings or rape.

• Annually, one in ten women is abused by the man with whom she lives.

• Repeated severe violence, estimated to occur in 1 in every 14 marriages, can cause long-term, disabling psychological trauma—the battered women's syndrome—similar to the trauma experienced by hostages or prisoners of war.

Unfortunately, women are not the only victims. Children are often the unintended victims of battering. Children in violent homes face dual threats: the threat of witnessing traumatic events, and the threat of physical assault. These experiences can transmit violence to the next generation. Steps to protect children and reduce the risk of intergenerational transmission of violent behavior include stronger laws, better training for criminal justice personnel, safe alternative housing coupled with social services, and prevention programs aimed at adolescents.

WITNESSING PARENTAL VIOLENCE

While most of us recognize immediately the harm inflicted by child abuse, the damage inflicted by living in a home with severe parent-to-parent violence is often overlooked. Although the extent of children's exposure to violence is poorly documented, children from violent families often provide clinicians with detailed accounts of abusive incidents their parents never realized they had witnessed. The immediate impact of this exposure can be traumatic—fear for self, fear for their mother's safety, and self-blame.

Even more troublesome is the likelihood that this exposure to

Cartoon by Steve Benson. Reprinted with permission of **Tribune Media Services**.

violence will lead to later violence on the part of the child–as well as to other serious emotional and behavioral problems. Violence witnessed at home is often repeated later in life. Violent parental conflict has been found in 20 to 40 percent of the families of chronically violent adolescents. These effects are particularly dismaying in view of the fact that at least 3.3 million children ages 3 to 17 are at risk of exposure to parental violence each year.

CHILD ABUSE

Violence between parents often extends to the children in the family as well. Physical abuse of at least one child has been found to occur in a large portion of battering incidents when children were present. Nearly 70% of the children of battered women surveyed in shelters had suffered physical abuse or neglect. Most of these children had been abused by the male batterer, but in a quarter of the cases, the children had been abused by both parents, and in a few cases by the mother alone. Battered women themselves are 8 times more likely to harm their children when they were being battered than when safe from violence.

THE EFFECTS OF FAMILY VIOLENCE

It is difficult, and sometimes impossible, to distinguish between the effects of witnessing parental violence and experiencing abuse as a child, due to the overlap in these problems. However, we do have ample evidence of the types of problems children from violent homes develop. They include high rates of fighting, delinquency, criminal violence, depression, suicidal behavior, phobias, and other physical and emotional disorders. The aggression that can appear in even very young child abuse victims tends to persist for a long time. With regard to delinquency, for example, over half the families reported for child abuse in one New York county later had at least one child appear in juvenile court.

RECOMMENDATIONS

There is much that can be done to reduce the violence in our homes, and there is no better investment for the future of this country. It is one of those root causes that, if ameliorated, can have long-term, lasting benefits. Top priorities should include:

1. Tougher law enforcement and sentencing to protect women and children and send the message that violence against women and children will not be tolerated. These should include, for example, strong penalties directed at violent offenders who cross state lines to assault or murder their partners and/or children in violation of a restraining order, by making this a federal offense. While relatively few in number, these offenders are among the

most dangerous.

2. Training for law enforcement officers, prosecutors, and judges in administering justice in family violence cases and responding appropriately to the special needs of these cases.

3. Access to safe housing coupled with social services to protect women and children, repair the damage of domestic violence, and avert homelessness prompted by desperate efforts to escape violent homes. This involves support for the greatest resource now available to battered women–grassroots shelters and advocacy organizations–as well as expanded access to federal, state and local programs that provide housing and social services.

4. Violence prevention programs in high schools and on campuses that deal with date rape, sexual harassment, and conflict resolution skills during the time when relationships and families of the future are being formed.

8   YOUTH VIOLENCE IN AMERICA: AN OVERVIEW

GUN MAYHEM AND ITS BURDEN ON THE HEALTH CARE SYSTEM

Paul McEnroe

Paul McEnroe is a staff writer for the Star Tribune *of Minneapolis. The following article was part of a* Star Tribune *six-part series on gun violence called "Bullets & Blood."*

Points to Consider:

1. Explain the relationship between gun violence and medical cost.

2. Who should pay the medical cost of gun violence in America?

3. What happened to Silas Coleman?

4. Who is Daniel Moynihan and what plan does he suggest?

5. Why does the National Rifle Association oppose the Moynihan plan?

Last year alone, the cost of caring for people who died from gunshots and who were injured by firearms in the United States was $2.7 billion.

After surviving another night of what the bullets did—setting his body afire with fever, filling his lungs with mucus—Silas Coleman gathered what reserves he had left and spoke with his eyes. Alongside the hospital bed where Coleman lay paralyzed from the nose down, his brother Kenneth held a plastic board full of letters, his fingers poised to turn the letters into words at his brother's direction. "This one?" asked Kenneth, his finger moving to one letter, waiting for his brother to respond, reading his face and patiently waiting to build the thought. If Silas wanted the letter, he raised his eyebrows. If not, he looked down and tightly closed his eyes.

Finally, the job was done. The 21-year-old quadriplegic was exhausted. His letter board read: "JUST GLAD TO BE ALIVE." In the millisecond it took for a bullet to sever his spinal cord on an October night in Minneapolis, Coleman became a statistic in what is a growing part of the nation's health care crisis: the epidemic of violence, particularly from handguns, and its overwhelming burden on the health care system.

COSTING BILLIONS

It is an epidemic seemingly without cure, especially frustrating because it is avoidable, not like a cancer or a crippling virus. And while the violence spirals upward, and as greater medical expertise is gained in treating people torn apart by bullets, a more frightening aspect of handgun violence is evolving: There are more and more Silas Colemans, young people who will live for years at a cost of billions of dollars borne by taxpayers and insurers.

"We just got an update on Silas' medical bill," said his father, Horace Harper, sitting in the hospital cafeteria an hour after leaving his son's room one day in mid-November. "It's already climbing over $91,000...and it will be weeks before they can even think of moving Silas out of the hospital. I guess Medicaid picks all this up, don't you think? Because Silas doesn't have any insurance."

By the time Coleman was transferred on Dec. 13 to Bethesda Lutheran Hospital and Rehabilitation Center in St. Paul, his bill at

49

Cartoon by Steve Sack. Reprinted with permission from **Star Tribune,** Minneapolis.

Hennepin County Medical Center was $203,961.42. Spit out of a computer printer, the document was more than 2 inches thick, consisting of more than 150 pages of single-line itemizations. By the end of a decade, the most conservative estimate for Coleman's medical care–without inflation–will be more than $3.6 million. It will all be paid by taxpayers.

NEW DEBATE

Coleman's very survival–viewed by doctors as nothing short of miraculous but devastating for what his future holds–has made him part of the equation in the new debate over whether hand-guns, ammunition and gun dealers should be heavily taxed to help pay the medical costs caused by firearms violence.

Last year alone, the cost of caring for people who died from gunshots and who were injured by firearms in the United States was $2.7 billion. By comparison, civilian firearm sales were about $2.1 billion. Ammunition sales were about $1 billion. Raising the taxes on arms and ammunition to help pay for the medical and social costs of violence could raise considerable money to help cover the costs of shooting victims such as Coleman, according to members of Congress who are pushing the idea.

But the numbers mean nothing when it's your child in the bed in front of you. As Silas Coleman's mother, Lois, read her son's words on his message board, only two sounds could be heard coming from the second-floor room in the intensive care ward at Hennepin County Medical Center. There was the rhythmic, soft hissing and suction sound of the electronic ventilator pumping oxygen through plastic tubes attached by a plug to the hole cut into Coleman's throat.

And mixing in was the crying coming up from his mother's throat, a sound of affirmation that her decision–it had been hers alone–to keep her son alive had been correct. That it had been right to refuse the option offered by doctors who could have put "Do Not Resuscitate" on Coleman's chart and let him die rather than keep him alive on a sophisticated heart-lung machine. But it is the cost of just such a decision that goes to the heart of the debate over increasing the taxes on guns and ammunition: With shootings increasing and affecting the uninsured poor more than any other group, who should pay the costs of keeping victims alive?

TRAGIC CASE

Dr. Galen Rockswold, the head of Hennepin County Medical Center's neurosurgery department, sat in his office one day last fall reviewing Coleman's case, which he considers to be the worst gunshot case he's encountered in nearly 20 years as a physician. "It's the most tragic injury there is for a young, healthy person like this because he's fully aware," said the 52-year-old doctor, letting his tall, thin frame slip down into his high-backed chair. "It just blows you away...and philosophically, each person has to ask himself the question whether it's worth living if this is the quality of my life..."

"There's no doubt it's a hard question, not only in the expense and the economic issues, but in the pain and suffering–can you imagine being the father of the son down there? That's something you can't measure."

"Treating somebody like this doesn't make economic sense, but you can't look at it that way. You can't play God."

"He says on the letter board, 'Glad to be alive.' To me, that shows Silas clearly represents somebody with extraordinary spirit and why you have to individualize this."

"You know, we're a country founded on strong individual rights...ah, I can't get going, it's too emotional."

He stopped, gathered himself while rocking back in the leather chair, then continued. "Rights, freedoms, belief in oneself. That's what's kept us strong in this country. I'm a hunter myself, and I'd gladly wait six months before being able to buy a shotgun. But we've reached a point in our society where those things are being turned upside down. I don't think an individual's right to bear arms is an adequate rationale for what we're seeing, because it's a society now out of control. Silas is the perfect example." "How many more Silases do you need, before it becomes a moral imperative you do something about handguns?"

BULLETS SENT A MESSAGE

Because of its brutality and the message behind it, Coleman's shooting Oct. 9 was big news in the Twin Cities for two days last fall. But it quickly faded from the public's mind. The following weekend, 14 people were admitted to Hennepin County Medical Center's emergency room for treatment of gunshot wounds. Coleman was shot nine times at the corner of 16th St. and James Av. N. in Minneapolis. That it happened outside North High School during the homecoming dance, in front of scores of people, would have usually made the attempted murder noteworthy. But the shooting—still unsolved despite eyewitnesses—was especially significant for another reason.

Two days earlier, Coleman had testified in an attempted murder trial. A friend had been wounded in what police were calling a gang-related drive-by shooting, and Coleman, not associated with any gangs himself, had seen it happen. He quickly received an unmistakable message from the street: Witnesses risk their lives if they show up in court to talk about gang activity.

The message was delivered this way: Three of the nine small-caliber bullets were shot into Silas' neck, the rest going into his chest, leg and hip. One of the three bullets in the neck severed the spinal cord, passing cleanly through the spinal canal just below his brain stem. It cut all the major nerves controlling movement from below the nose.

When paramedics arrived, they found Coleman had been carrying a .380 handgun. "I wasn't surprised or angry when I found that out," said his father, Horace Harper. "Silas knew he needed some sort of protection against the kind of message he was likely to get on the street for testifying. It's a fact of life out there you need protection for yourself, especially when the police can't offer any worthwhile protection to him for what he did."

GUN LAWS

Ten days after the shooting, in Washington, DC, a city where such shootings get little attention, the chairman of the Finance Committee of the U.S. Senate, Sen. Daniel Moynihan, convened a hearing by rattling a box of brass cartridges. It was an appropriate opening: The New York Democrat had called the hearing to discuss the consequences of social behavior on health care, with emphasis on guns and violence.

Moynihan sees those brass projectiles as the cornerstone of a plan to pay for handgun violence, possibly as part of President Clinton's health care plan. Moynihan advocates imposing a 10,000 percent tax on hollow-point bullets, raising the cost from about $20 a box to $4,000. Hollow-points blossom into razor-sharp projectiles on impact, ricocheting off body parts and causing massive damage. He wants only the police and military to have access to the bullets, which are famed for their "knock-down" power.

There could be support for Moynihan's proposal in Minnesota. A Minnesota Poll found that two-thirds of the state's adults, 68 percent, favor stricter controls on the availability of ammunition as a way of reducing violent crime. With more than 200 million guns in the country, the idea of being able to gain control over them is almost pointless, Moynihan said. His position is that if Congress doesn't have the guts to tighten handgun laws, why not heavily tax what's put into the guns and use most of that revenue in health care, especially for trauma caused by violence?

The National Rifle Association (NRA) opposes Moynihan's proposals, saying that gun control activists are now using the health care crisis to attack the rights of people to bear arms. The NRA opposes any tax increase on firearms or ammunition, and says the solution to violence is to give criminals longer sentences and to enforce the firearms possession laws already on the books.

In 1992, more than 14,500 murders were committed with guns in the United States, compared with 186 in Canada, where guns are strictly regulated. In Hennepin County in 1992, there were 75 homicides, 38 of them by firearms. In Ramsey County last year, there were 29 homicides and 23 of them were by guns.

NATIONAL FIGURES

The latest national figures from the Centers for Disease Control and Prevention (CDC) in Atlanta, Ga., show that of the 102,300 people wounded by gunshots in 1990–the latest available figures–64 percent were sent to the emergency room and 58 percent required hospitalization. And then there is the group Silas Coleman falls into. Of the wounded who were hospitalized, the CDC found that 17 percent had primary injuries to the head and neck area–more than 10,000 people. The low figure on lifetime care costs for quadriplegia is $600,000–although Coleman's care will cost the system millions more.

"People in this condition can live for decades, easily into their 40s and 50s if they don't succumb to infection," said nurse Peg Arveson, the clinical manager of the respiratory unit at Bethesda, the rehabilitation center where Coleman now lives. "That's the cost of guns and violence for just one person. That's what modern medical technology has given us without consideration to the quality of life it leaves."

INTERPRETING EDITORIAL CARTOONS

This activity may be used as an individualized study guide for students in libraries and resource centers or as a discussion catalyst in small group and classroom discussions.

Although cartoons are usually humorous, the main intent of most political cartoonists is not to entertain. Cartoons express serious social comment about important issues. Using graphic and visual arts, the cartoonist expresses opinions and attitudes. By employing an entertaining and often light-hearted visual format, cartoonists may have as much or more impact on national and world issues as editorial and syndicated columnists.

Points to Consider

1. Examine the cartoon on page 50.

2. How would you describe the message of the cartoon? Try to describe the message in one to three sentences.

3. Do you agree with the message expressed in the cartoon? Why or why not?

4. Does the cartoon support the author's point of view in any of the readings in this publication? If the answer is yes, be specific about which reading or readings and why.

5. Are any of the readings in Chapter One in basic agreement with the cartoon?

CHAPTER 2

VIOLENCE IN SCHOOLS

9   VIOLENCE IN SCHOOLS

SCHOOL VIOLENCE:
AN OVERVIEW

Madeleine Kunin

Madeleine Kunin wrote the following article as deputy secretary of the United States Department of Education.

Points to Consider:

1. How extensive is violence in American schools?

2. When and where are firearms present in schools?

3. How often are teachers assaulted?

4. How often do students fight?

5. How often are students killed?

Excerpted from testimony by Madeleine Kunin before the Subcommittee on Education, Arts and Humanities of the Senate Committee on Labor and Human Resources, September 23, 1993.

Our children and parents are increasingly worried about safety.

These days things are different. Our children and parents are increasingly worried about safety. The opening of school signals not only the traditional start of the formal learning cycle, for many it also represents the start of the worrying cycle: worrying not only about whether a child is going to do well in school, but also whether a child will get to school and return home without being threatened, assaulted, or even killed; worrying about whether the next phone call will be from the school, the police, or the emergency room.

And parents–be they from urban, suburban, or rural areas, affluent or poor–have every right to be worried, for the fact is that many of our schools are disruptive and violent acts do occur. In many of our schools gang activity, vandalism, theft, sexual harassment, and assault have become commonplace. Weapons are commonplace, too, including guns. It is clear that education and violence do not mix, that we cannot ask parents to accept violence as an everyday hazard of sending their child to school.

Let me give you a few examples of incidents that have already occurred:

• **New Salem, Pennsylvania:** An 11-year old girl was abducted from a school bus stop at knife point and tied to a tree where she stayed for more than two days until she was able to free herself. The child then walked five miles and hid in the weeds overnight before making it to a trailer home and calling her mother.

• **Washington, DC:** A 14-year old youth was held on charges that he and another young male allegedly fired at least 15 shots outside Shaw Junior High School as classes ended. No one was injured, but on the second day of classes the incident had students running for cover.

• **Atlanta, Georgia:** A ninth-grade student at Atlanta's Harper High School died after being shot in a crowded lunchroom by another student with whom he had been feuding for months. Another 10th-grader was wounded in the shooting.

• **Los Angeles, California:** A 15-year old boy, an innocent bystander to an argument, was shot and critically wounded at Dorsey High School when an argument broke out between three youths and another youth.

"ANY CHANCE the U.N. will SEND PEACE KEEPERS?"

Cartoon by David Catrow. Reprinted with permission of **Coply News Service.**

- **Dallas, Texas:** A 15-year old student was fatally shot by a fellow student in a crowded hallway at Roosevelt High School. The student was shot at point blank range in what police called a continuing dispute. A 16-year old youth was arrested for the killing.

If prior years are any indication of what we can expect in this school year, incidents such as these are likely to recur unless we take some immediate action. If we fail to take action we can expect to see:

- *Students reluctant to go to school or transferring schools because of fear of violence.*

A recent survey found that overall 37 percent of students don't feel safe in school. This is double the number found in a similar survey conducted in 1989. The survey also found that 50 percent of students know someone who switched schools to feel safer; 43 percent of public school students avoid school restrooms; 20 percent avoid hallways; and 45 percent avoid the school grounds (*USA Today Weekend* August 13-15, 1993).

- *Weapons being taken from students, some as young as 7 and 8 years old.*

Another survey found that 59 percent of the students surveyed nationwide said guns were easily obtainable, while 35 percent said it would take them less than 60 minutes to get one. The survey also found that more than one in five (22 percent) students claimed they carried a weapon to school during the last school year (survey conducted by the Louis Harris Corporation, prepared for the Harvard School of Public Health, July 1993). These findings are consistent with the findings of the Centers for Disease Control and Prevention (CDC) which reported that nearly 20 percent of all students in grades 9-12 said they had carried a weapon at least once during the 30 days preceding the survey. Male students (31.5 percent) were much more likely than female students (8.1 percent) to report having carried a weapon (CDC's 1990-1991 Youth Risk Behavior Surveillance System).

• *Fights*

Nearly 8 percent of all students in grades 9-12 reported that during the 30 days preceding the survey they had been in at least one physical fight, though not always at school, that resulted in an injury requiring treatment by a doctor or nurse (CDC's 1990-1991 Youth Risk Behavior Surveillance System).

• *Gangs*

Fifteen percent of the students said their school had gangs (Department of Justice, Bureau of Justice Statistics).

• *Students injured and sexually assaulted.*

Nearly 3 million thefts and violent crimes occur on or near school campuses every year. This equates to almost 16,000 incidents per school day, or one every six seconds. 1.9 million of these incidents are considered violent crimes, and they include rape, robbery, assault, and murder (Department of Justice, Bureau of Justice Statistics).

- *Teachers being assaulted*

Nearly one out of five public school teachers reported being verbally abused by students in the 30 days before the survey, eight percent reported being physically threatened, and two percent reported being physically assaulted during the year (Department of Education, Fast Response Survey).

- *More students killed*

Although national records are not kept, data from the National School Safety Center indicate that approximately 30 persons were killed in schools, on their way to schools, or on school property during the last school year. I can go on and provide you with many more statistics and stories related to violence in our schools. I want, however, to direct my remarks not to the negative aspects of violence and what is occurring in some of our schools, but on our beliefs and our expectations for schools. We believe that:

- Violence is not an everyday occurrence in most of our schools.

- We can provide our children with the skills necessary to cope with conflict, in the school or community, in a nonviolent manner.

- With hard work, outreach to the community, appropriate training, and provision of needed resources we can change the environment in which children learn. We can create an environment that is free of drugs, free of disruptive behavior, and free of violence.

THE SAFE SCHOOL ACT:
Points and Counterpoints

Edward M. Kennedy vs. Colman McCarthy

Edward M. Kennedy is a United States Senator from Massachusetts and a prominent leader in Congress and the nation. Colman McCarthy is a nationally syndicated columnist.

Points to Consider:

1. How is the Safe Schools Act defined by Senator Kennedy?

2. Why does he support it?

3. How is the Safe School Act defined by Colman McCarthy?

4. Why does he oppose it?

5. Can you find any similarities between the two authors in their approach to school violence?

EDWARD M. KENNEDY: The Point

The rising tide of violence in our schools continues unabated. According to the National Crime Survey, almost 3 million crimes occur on or near school campuses every year–that is 16,000 every school day, or one every six seconds.

The Safe Schools Act of 1993 is an aggressive new program to help free our schools of the violence that has turned so many of our classrooms into war zones. The Act would provide funds to local school districts to help achieve the sixth National Education Goal to eliminate drugs and violence in our elementary and secondary schools, so that by the year 2000, every school child in this country will be able to receive an education without the fear of violence.

It is the first-ever comprehensive federal program to provide funds directly to local school districts to develop and implement plans to reduce and prevent the occurrence of violence in schools. The Safe Schools Act allows local school districts the flexibility to design their own programs while at the same time, supporting national leadership activities. A demonstration project such as the National Model City Project is twofold in its purpose: not only would it provide funds for planning and implementation at the local level, but would provide a model that schools and communities around the nation could emulate.

EDUCATION

The Safe Schools Act underscores the importance of education prevention programs to teach our students to deal with conflict in a non-violent manner. Unfortunately, security devices such as metal detectors have become all too necessary in many of our schools. In fact, according to the National School Safety Center, approximately one quarter of our nation's big-city school systems currently use metal detectors to stem the flow of weapons into the schools. While the bill does not negate their utility and importance, it encourages schools to make metal detectors and the hiring of security part of a long-term, comprehensive effort, focusing on preventive education with programs such as peer mediation and conflict resolution.

NATIONAL PRIORITY

Although some schools in our country have made efforts to curb

Cartoon by Mike Keefe.

the problem of violence in schools, whether it be via metal detectors or conflict resolution programs, the incidents and statistics on violence demand that school safety become a national priority. The United States faces a crisis in its effort to provide a world-class education for all. Teachers cannot teach and students cannot learn in an environment filled with fear and intimidation. Acts of violence disrupt the normal functioning of a school, and fear of violence prevents students and teachers from concentrating on meaningful learning and teaching. The Longfellow School in Bridgeport, Connecticut, has installed bullet-proof glass to keep children from becoming targets of stray bullets. Our schools cannot afford to become fortresses. The Safe Schools Act adopted by the Committee makes school safety a national priority. We cannot stall the effort to provide our students with world-class education by denying them the safety of their own lives in the classrooms and hallways of the schools in our nation.

Passage of the Safe Schools Act is a first step, but is not the only step to ensuring a comprehensive strategy to address school violence. The expansion of the Drug-Free Schools and Communities Act to include not only drug abuse prevention education, but violence prevention as well, is needed to address the multiple and often duplicative risk factors that often draw students to alcohol and drug use and violent behavior. As part of the reauthorization of the Elementary and Secondary Education Act, a more comprehensive Safe and Drug-Free Schools and Communities Act can provide our schools with some of the tools necessary to insure that we, as a nation, achieve the 6th National Education Goal, that every school in America will be free of drugs and violence and will offer a disciplined environment conducive to learning.

Concern with school violence is not new. It was first brought to national attention in the 1970s, largely through the efforts of the Bayh Committee hearings and the 1978 Safe School Study sponsored by the National Institute of Education. The Safe Schools Act of 1993 brings the crucial problem of school violence to the forefront in the 1990s where it will gain the attention it merits and provide the impetus to achieve safety for all our children in every school by the year 2000 and beyond.

COLMAN MCCARTHY: The Counterpoint

Were I a full-time public school teacher, I imagine my reaction to the proposed Safe Schools Act would be this: I'm paid to teach, and I want to teach, but I also act as a social worker, psychiatrist, entertainer, dad, self-esteem builder, clergyman, letter-of-recommendation writer and disciplinarian. And now Education Secretary Richard Riley; who is calling for the $175 million Safe Schools Act, meant to provide grants to combat school crime and violence, has still another role: cop.

WEALTH AND POVERTY

My alarm would be major or minor depending on the wealth of the taxpayers whose children I teach. An educator in a wealthy school district with a tax base that provides $8,500 per student a year is not likely to be shot, knifed or slugged by the estimated one out of five high school students who carry weapons. Those kids are mostly in impoverished schools where the outlay is $2,500 and where decaying neighborhoods mean that violence in the streets and homes spills into the schools.

The Safe Schools Act, now before the House Subcommittee on Elementary, Secondary and Vocational Education, requires that the money go to "school districts most troubled by high rates of crime and violence." As much as one-third of the funds–$58 million–can be used for metal detectors and security guards, with the rest available for schools to devise their own safety or violence-prevention programs.

NEW SOLUTIONS

New thinking, not a new law, is needed. This is the first federal response to what many local districts have been overwhelmed by for years. Nearly $60 million for disarming punks and expanding law enforcement is not an educational solution. The desperate environment of kids gunning down teachers, or each other, is an invitation for schools to expand the curriculum to give students a full academic grounding in the skills and theories of nonviolent conflict resolution. This would be a breakthrough to a positive kind of violence prevention, not the negative kind found in metal detectors and hallway police.

Riley, the educator, not Riley the criminologist, is aware that the classroom is where genuine solutions are to be found. In a recent speech at a two-day Washington conference on violence prevention, he argued that "We need comprehensive programs that address a host of 'risk factors' that our students come to school with, and we need to provide them with the skills necessary to deal with conflict in a nonviolent manner."

Not bad, considering that previous secretaries avoided the issue. Still it was cautious. In the same speech, Riley praised George McKenna, the former principal of a gang-ridden Los Angeles high school and now superintendent of the Inglewood school district. McKenna has been advocating that "conflict resolution be taught at all grade levels" and "a nonviolence curriculum be made mandatory in all California schools." Riley had an opportunity to endorse those ideas and call for them nationally. Instead he singled out McKenna only for getting parents involved in their troubled local high school.

PEACE EDUCATION

The question about Riley and his staff is how serious are they about bringing a federal presence to peace education. No further studies are needed to document the depths of the crime and violence epidemic. Everyone from the American Medical Association to the Justice Department has weighed in with gloomy facts and the inevitable calls for action. Fighting ignorance, not crime, is the role of schools.

To graduate students who are ignorant in the techniques, history and literature of nonviolent conflict resolution is to leave them helpless before life's inevitable disputes, whether among families, groups or governments. It abandons them to be one-sidedly educated by other childhood teachers–from television violence, war toys and perhaps parents who abuse each other to national leaders who think air strikes and bombing people bring peace.

Such national organizations as the Resolving Conflict Creatively Program in New York and the Peace Education Foundation in Miami can document that classroom teaching of peacemaking does reduce violence. If the Department of Education wants a federal role for itself, it should hold off on the Safe Schools Act and look at the Higher Education Amendments of 1992. This authorized $350 million for 1993 and four succeeding years for teacher training, including "training aimed at resolving conflicts." No money was appropriated by Congress for this law.

11   VIOLENCE IN SCHOOLS

GUN-FREE SCHOOL ZONES:
Points and Counterpoints

Edward P. Kovacic and Jay Baker

Edward P. Kovacic and Jay Baker made the following comments while testifying before a Congressional committee on the subject of creating Gun-Free Zones around all American schools. Edward P. Kovacic testified as Chief of Police for the City of Cleveland. Jay Baker testified as the Director of Legislative Action for the National Rifle Association.

The Gun-Free School Zone Act, debated below, was declared unconstitutional by a federal appeals court saying the law did not comply with the Constitutions Commerce Clause, which allows Congress to regulate interstate commerce. The Clinton Administration then asked the United States Supreme Court to overturn this appeals court decision and to reinstate the federal ban on possession of guns within 1,000 feet of schools.

Points to Consider:

1. Compare and contrast the way Kovacic and Baker define the Gun-Free School Zone Act.

2. Why does Jay Baker oppose it?

3. Why does Edward P. Kovacic favor it?

Excerpted from arguments by Edward P. Kovacic and Jay Baker before the Subcommittee on Crime of the House Committee on the Judiciary, September 6, 1990.

JAY BAKER: The Point

At a time when federal resources are stretched to the breaking point and many potential cases against career criminals and felons in possession of firearms are not being made, H.R. 3757 preempts the states by creating a new federal offense in duplication of or overriding many existing state statutes. There is no state in which the carrying of a loaded firearm with criminal intent is not a crime—whether within the boundaries of an arbitrarily designated school zone or on a public street. Unless Congress intends to establish and fund a "Federal School Patrol Division" within the Bureau of Alcohol, Tobacco and Firearms or within the Department of Justice—something the NRA would join the ACLU in adamantly opposing—H.R. 3757 will remain a political exercise completely devoid of any impact on public safety or the lives of our children. It is not at all surprising that this hearing comes only two months from the general elections. It is a symbolic gesture which will punish no serious criminals but will likely wreck the lives of a few honest citizens caught in a carelessly prepared and ineptly cast net.

FLAWED LEGISLATION

This legislation is patterned after the "drug-free school zones" measure, but the analogy is flawed. The "drug-free school zones" statute makes a more serious federal crime of what is already a crime in all fifty states and the District of Columbia, as well as at the federal level. H.R. 3757 creates a new federal offense, and one which may not be an offense at the state level. Indeed, it may be taking what the state constitution interprets as a guaranteed right and making it a federal felony. The drug-free school zone concept attacks something generally outlawed—drug possession—and makes it a more serious felony. The gun-free school zone elevates something which is generally lawful, indeed constitutionally protected—firearms possession—to the level of a serious federal felony under certain circumstances.

TWO AREAS

There are two areas in which this bill could have an impact. First, it could provide grounds to prosecute otherwise law-abiding citizens who are transporting firearms in compliance with state and local law—but in violation of this new federal proposal. Second, it appears to give new powers to public schools, powers previously held by the state or by the locality in which the school is located. We are unaware of many other fields in which public school officials have been given the authority to regulate–either restrictively or leniently–activities in an area up to 1,000 feet from the grounds of a public school. Yet H.R. 3757 appears to permit the possession of a gun within a public school zone–but not on school property.

While there are thus two good reasons to continue to leave the regulation of firearms carrying and transportation to the states by rejecting H.R. 3757, several amendments could lessen the dangers this legislation poses to law-abiding firearms owners. Our principal concern is the potential prosecution of parents who unwittingly violate the provisions of a new federal law while dropping their children off at school on the way to the range or a hunt. The drafters of H.R. 3757 may not realize that their exemption for a "locked firearms rack" makes little sense considering most, if not all, firearms racks are not equipped with locks nor designed in a way that makes addition of a padlock a practical alternative.

THE NRA RECOMMENDS THE FOLLOWING AMENDMENTS:

* Prosecution should require a willful violation.

* The penalty should be a misdemeanor that does not prohibit otherwise law-abiding citizens from owning firearms as a felony conviction would. This will not permit serious criminals to escape as other felony charges will be available.

* The exemptions should be clarified by making it a bar to federal prosecution if the transporting or carrying was not unlawful under state or local law.

* Finally, considerations of due process require appropriate notice through posting. Signs should be posted on a perimeter approximately 1,000 feet from each of the nation's 80,000 public schools on each street at that point. A sign near a school announcing a "Gun-Free School Zone" with another sign indicating "End School Zone" a few yards away would fail a due process test since the notice provided would be conflicting and confusing.

Reprinted with permission of **Tribune Media Services**.

EDWARD C. KOVACIC: The Counterpoint

I ask that Congress act with all due speed to ensure the safety of our children and their teachers while engaged in the vital process of education through passage of the Gun-Free School Zones Act.

In looking more closely at the incidents, it is observed that firearms have been employed in a wide variety of offenses in and around schools. Such offenses as felonious assault, aggravated robbery and aggravated menacing to kidnapping and rape, witness intimidation and child enticement have been recorded. In previous years, the possession and use of firearms came to the Division's attention mainly through the investigation of threats and assaults. We are now recording firearms being possessed by persons arrested in connection with the violation of state drug law offenses in and around schools.

HANDGUNS

The predominate firearm of choice in all classes of offenses is the handgun; however, there have been incidents recorded involving the use of shotguns and rifles. To illustrate, Cleveland police officers were fired upon from an elementary school yard. As a result, seven males were arrested and seven firearms were confiscated. Three of these firearms were shotguns and one was a rifle. Of the 203 incidents recorded, a total of 231 firearms were used.

As in the case of Congress, the Ohio Legislature has reacted to the school firearm problem by introducing Senate Bill 52 on January 24, 1989. Senate Bill 52 makes it a second degree felony punishable upon conviction for a period of incarceration of 2, 3, 4 or 5 years to 15 years for anyone found in possession of a firearm on school premises. It differs from the Gun-Free School Zone Act in that it applies only to firearm possession in schools or on school premises. The Gun-Free School Zone Act establishes a "zone" which extends 1000 feet in any direction from the school, and its coverage is broader and would more directly address the problem of "pushers" attempting to solicit drug sales among children in areas adjacent to school property while in possession of a firearm.

In addition to covering a wider geographic area than Senate Bill 52, the Act will serve as a potent deterrent to those who may contemplate engaging in armed criminal activity in and around schools. And for those who are not deterred and are arrested and convicted, the aggregate period of incarceration for state and federal offenses will keep them from committing any subsequent or like offenses for a considerable period of time. If the Gun-Free School Zones Act is enacted into law, I would promulgate a directive which would require that the local field office of the Bureau of Alcohol, Tobacco and Firearms be advised about any violation of this law.

CONCLUSION

In summary, conditions in Cleveland cannot be that different from the rest of our nation's cities. Over the past seven years, we have seen a marked, virtually continuous rise in the number of incidents involving firearms in or around school property. It is almost as if the purpose of our schools has changed; from a place devoted to education and preparing for the future to an open marketplace for drug dealers and those that prey upon children. Therefore, I urge you to act promptly and favorably to consider passage of the Gun-Free School Zones Act of 1990. You have the power to restore confidence in the ability of government to safeguard our children, our nation's most valuable resource. Passage of this Act will enable our children and their teachers to travel to and from and attend their schools without an overriding fear for their personal safety.

WHAT IS POLITICAL BIAS?

This activity may be used as an individualized study guide for students in libraries and resource centers or as a discussion catalyst in small group and classroom discussions.

Many readers are unaware that written material usually expresses an opinion or bias. The skill to read with insight and understanding requires the ability to detect different kinds of bias. **Political bias, race bias, sex bias, ethnocentric bias** and **religious bias** are five basic kinds of opinions expressed in editorials and literature that attempt to persuade. This activity will focus on **political bias** defined in the glossary below.

Five Kinds of Editorial Opinion or Bias

Sex Bias–the expression of dislike for and/or feeling of superiority over a person because of gender or sexual preference

Race Bias–the expression of dislike for and/or feeling of superiority over a racial group

Ethnocentric Bias–the expression of a belief that one's own group, race, religion, culture or nation is superior. Ethnocentric persons judge others by their own standards and values.

Political Bias–the expression of opinions and attitudes about government-related issues on the local, state, national or international level

Religious Bias–the expression of a religious belief or attitude

---

Guidelines

Read through the following statements and decide which ones represent **political opinion or bias**. Evaluate each statement by using the method indicated below.

- **Mark (P)** for statements that reflect any **political opinion or bias**.

- **Mark (O)** for statements that reflect other kinds of opinion or bias.

- **Mark (F)** for any factual statements.

- **Mark (N)** for any statements that you are not sure about.

_____ 1. Law enforcement alone cannot stem the tide of violence in the United States.

_____ 2. Homicide is now the leading cause of death among children in many American inner cities.

_____ 3. Government does not include enough incentives to prevent the development of dysfunctional families.

_____ 4. Children who witness violence in the home or community are scarred like the victims.

_____ 5. Children who commit violent crimes from the age of thirteen should be tried as adults.

_____ 6. The "social alternative" methods have not done the job in preventing crime.

_____ 7. Urban decay and lack of economic opportunity have helped to breed a generation of violence.

_____ 8. The breakdown of the family and traditional discipline can best explain the upswing of adolescent violence.

_____ 9. More and more elementary school students in urban areas have witnessed violent acts of crime.

_____ 10. Gangs give urban youth a chance to gain acceptance and family, something that they are lacking in their own homes.

_____ 11. The lenient attitude of the courts toward youth and crime has caused a generation to believe that they can literally "get away with murder."

_____ 12. The best way to crusade against crime is to be an active children's advocate.

_____ 13. Racial or ethnic background and crime rate have no correlation.

_____ 14. Parents must be a more powerful influence over children than television or peer groups.

_____ 15. Schools must intervene at the primary school level to teach non-violence and conflict resolution techniques.

Additional Activities

1. Locate three examples of **political opinion or bias** in the readings from Chapter Two.

2. Make up one-sentence statements that would be an example of each of the following: **sex bias, race bias, ethnocentric bias, and religious bias**.

CHAPTER 3

GANGS, GUNS, AND VIOLENCE

12 GANGS, GUNS, AND VIOLENCE

DEFINING YOUTH GANGS

Suzanne Cavanagh and David Teasley

Suzanne Cavanagh and David Teasley are analysts in the National Government. They wrote the following article for the Government Division of the Congressional Research Service.

Points to Consider:

1. How are gangs defined?

2. What characteristics do they share?

3. Distinguish between "gangs" and "delinquent" groups.

4. Describe the ethnic/racial make-up of gangs.

5. How do gangs spread from one city to another?

Suzanne Cavanagh and David Teasley, "Youth Gangs: An Overview," Congressional Research Service, June 9, 1992.

There is no generally agreed upon definition of youth gangs.

Since the 1960s, there has been little research on youth gangs. In an article discussing the most effective policies for gang reduction and control, Assistant Attorney General Jimmy Gurulé concludes that "little is known about what works in gang suppression, prevention, and intervention..." Similarly, social scientist John Hagedorn asserts that present understanding of youth gangs in the 1990s is limited in two ways. First, he concludes that very little empirical research on gangs has been done since the 1960s. Second, he argues that the research on gangs completed in the 1960s, when the bulk of the fieldwork was done, is no longer relevant to the gangs of the 1990s.

DEFINITION AND CHARACTERISTICS

There is no generally agreed upon definition of youth gangs among those studying the gang phenomena at the present time. Most researchers agree that not all delinquent groups are gangs. Analysts attempting to distinguish between gangs and delinquent groups point out that the two exhibit different types of deviance. For example, delinquent groups tend to be more loosely organized. By contrast, youth gangs appear to be more cohesive. Both groups engage in a range of crimes, but youth gangs are reportedly more violent. Unlike members of delinquent youth groups, gang members tend to be somewhat older and share more characteristics such as age, race, sex, and neighborhood homogeneity.

Sociologists Malcolm Klein and Cheryl Maxson, who are on the faculty of the University of Southern California and affiliated with the University's Social Science Research Institute, offer a definition of a youth gang as a group of teenagers and young adults who:

(a) are generally perceived as a distinct aggregation by others in their neighborhood, (b) recognize themselves as a denotable group (almost invariably with a group name) and (c) have been involved in a sufficient number of [illegal] incidents to call forth a consistent negative response from neighborhood residents and/or enforcement agencies...

Members of youth gangs share characteristics of age, sex, and ethnicity/race. The age range is broad–from just under 10 years

Cartoon by Mike Ramirez. Reprinted with permission of **Coply News Service**.

old to slightly over 50 years, with the average age for gang offenders identified as 19.4 years in a recent study. Current research indicates that members are remaining in gangs and not "maturing out" as rapidly as they once did. While there may be many explanations for this, analysts John Hagedorn and Perry Macon, who did field research interviewing gang members in Milwaukee, Wisconsin, attribute the failure of youths to "mature out" of gangs to the urban underclass theory. Underclass theory, according to one author:

postulates a new social class created by a new set of demographic, technological, and economic conditions whereby the demand for low-skilled workers in an increasingly service-oriented high-tech economy has been reduced drastically, permanently locking them out of the labor market and cutting off upward mobility routes available to earlier generations.

Most youth gangs consist of males, although there is a small number of all female gangs. Male gang members reportedly commit a larger proportion of violent crimes than do their female counterparts. According to a 1988 study conducted by the Chicago Police, only 2 percent of gang offenders over a period of a year and a half were females. This percentage has remained consistent over several decades.

VIOLENCE

The inclination to violence springs from the circumstances of life among the ghetto poor–the lack of jobs that pay a living wage, the stigma of race, the fallout from rampant drug use and drug trafficking, and the resulting alienation and lack of hope for the future.

Elijah Anderson, "The Code of the Streets," **The Atlantic Monthly**, May, 1994.

Current studies indicate that gang members are predominantly black or Hispanic. A 1989 Department of Justice survey estimated that youth gang membership nationally was approximately 50 percent black, 35 percent Hispanic, and the remaining 15 percent white or Asian. Los Angeles police department statistics on gangs in 1991 showed 257 gangs were black, 240 Hispanic, 44 Asian, and 4 white. Though there are fewer Asian gangs than black or Hispanic gangs, the former are growing at a rapid rate. Many policy-makers and law enforcement officials predict that Chinese-organized crime groups will become the leading organized crime problem of the 1990s.

SPREAD OF GANGS

A recent phenomenon of the gang problem is the spread of gangs nationwide. Originally located on the East and West Coasts, gangs are now found in the Midwest and South. Moreover, gangs were once a problem of primarily large urban areas; today gangs exist in cities with populations as small as 8,000.

There is disagreement as to whether the spread of gangs involves the linkage of one gang to another. A case in point is the alleged migration of two Los Angeles street gangs, the Crips and the Bloods. The Department of Justice maintains that gangs with links to the Crips and Bloods have appeared in nearly all of the 50 States. Others present an opposing view, suggesting that the migration of Crips and Bloods has been greatly exaggerated. Another researcher who studied gangs in Milwaukee argues that although small city youth gangs pattern themselves after their larger urban counterparts, there is little evidence to suggest that large city gangs establish units or chapters in smaller cities.

13   GANGS, GUNS, AND VIOLENCE

GUNS AND GANGS IN PUBLIC HOUSING: PROS AND CONS

Edward Walsh

Edward Walsh wrote the following article for the Washington Post.

Points to Consider:

1. What are the Robert Taylor Homes?

2. How is the state of public housing described?

3. Define the legal battle over safety and constitutional rights in public housing.

4. Summarize the meaning of "Operation Clean Sweep."

Edward Walsh, "Guns in Public Housing Force Showdown of Rights vs. Needs," **Washington Post**, December 26, 1993. © 1993 **Washington Post**. Reprinted with permission.

Last summer, several young housing authority tenants fell from open windows of high-rise buildings and some died.

Dozens of law-enforcement officers, looking for weapons, swept into several high-rise buildings at the Robert Taylor Homes public housing project in Chicago last summer. They did not have search warrants, and the man in charge, Housing Authority Police Chief Hosea Crossley, admitted that the searches technically were illegal. "We're in an emergency situation out here," Crossley said at the time. "Anytime you're prevented from installing measures to save lives because of some young punks with guns, it's an emergency."

LEGAL BATTLE

The weapon sweeps at Robert Taylor Homes and other public housing developments in Chicago have reignited a longstanding legal battle over the safety and constitutional rights of residents of one of the nation's larger and more troubled public housing systems.

On one side is the American Civil Liberties Union (ACLU), representing several housing authority tenants who charged in a lawsuit filed in federal court last month that the weapon searches trampled the rights of public housing residents to be secure in their own homes. Residents of luxury, high-rise apartments lining Chicago's lakefront would not be expected to tolerate such intrusions and public housing tenants should be treated no differently, ACLU lawyers argued. "There really is only one Constitution, and the beauty of the model is it applies to everyone," said Harvey Grossman, the ACLU's legal director in Chicago.

On the other side are Chicago Housing Authority officials, claiming support of the vast majority of their tenants, who say the grim reality of life in crime-infested buildings justifies extraordinary measures to combat heavily armed gangs. "You can't compare life in Robert Taylor and Henry Horner [another housing project] to life in Lake Forest," a wealthy Chicago suburb, housing authority chairman Vince Lane said. "The majority of people in these communities say they didn't have any rights before 1988; the gangs took them all...I'd like to see Harvey live in Robert Taylor. I'd bet he'd ask for the Marines, not security."

Cartoon by Gary Markstein.

HOUSING AUTHORITY

The setting for this dispute is bleakly modern, towering and foreboding housing authority buildings where drugs and gunfire are part of everyday life. But the issues involved are as ageless as the conflict between individual liberty and social order. Soon after becoming housing authority chairman in 1988, Lane said, he learned that a 7-year-old girl had been burned severely when a Molotov cocktail was thrown into her family's public housing apartment. "I realized that no matter how many management improvements I made, I would never be able to implement them because we didn't control the buildings," he said.

CLEAN SWEEP

Lane soon launched "Operation Clean Sweep," a massive undertaking that attracted national attention. After police secured building perimeters, housing authority inspection teams entered the buildings, rooting out illegal tenants, checking the physical condition of apartments and issuing photo-identification cards to legal residents.

The ACLU, representing a few housing authority buildings, sued to stop "Operation Clean Sweep," charging that the "inspections" actually were illegal, warrantless "searches" and that the housing authority was illegally restricting visitor access. After lengthy negotiations, the two sides agreed to a court-approved consent decree in 1989. Under it, the housing authority agreed to stop demanding that people entering the buildings produce identification and to restrict sweeps to cases involving an "immediate threat" to the safety of tenants or property.

A TRUCE

For the next three years, the ACLU and housing authority observed a truce. But then two dramatic events intervened, sending the two sides back to court. One was the death in October 1992 of Dantrell Davis, 7, struck by sniper fire as he walked to school with his mother from their home in the Cabrini-Green public housing complex. In the ensuing uproar, housing authority lawyers asked that the consent decree be modified to allow them to resume demanding identification of everyone entering the buildings and to install metal detectors at entrances. While that case is pending, the housing authority has installed metal detectors in most buildings, which Grossman contended "raised serious constitutional issues," because an apartment, even in a public housing complex, is not the same as an airport or a courthouse.

Last summer, several young housing authority tenants fell from open windows of high-rise buildings and some died. It seemed, Lane said, that it was "raining children." In response, Lane began an emergency program to install window guards. But when crews arrived at Robert Taylor Homes in August, gang members drove them away with gunfire. That incident, Lane testified at a court hearing, persuaded him to adopt a "firm policy" of responding to random gunfire with massive weapon searches.

TENANT SUPPORT

Artensa Randolph, head of an advisory board composed of presidents of tenant councils in each housing authority complex, said tenants strongly support the sweeps. Life in public housing, she said, "is a little better" since Lane began the security crackdown five years ago. Before then, Randolph said, "we had to pay [gang members] to get our groceries upstairs. Where was the ACLU then?"

Said Grossman: "The question here is the choice of weapons. How do you fight crime? The housing authority has shown a willingness to try short cuts around the Constitution. We believe ade-

LIKE A JUNGLE

Before the guards came along, "it was just like a jungle," says Dorothy M. Dean, 70 years old and a Geneva resident for 27 years. She now wanders the project freely, day or night. "The security they got now, I'm so pleased," she says. "If they got rid of the security here, I'd be ready to leave."

Jim Carlton, "Project Residents Gain Freedom from Crime," **The Wall Street Journal**, 1994.

quate, competent law enforcement is the answer. We don't want less security. We want more security." Grossman said that in addition to the housing authority's 350-member police force, Chicago police should be redeployed to put more officers in high-crime areas, which include most public housing developments. "If serious, violent crime is the most significant issue we have to deal with, serious, violent crime should be the primary factor in the assignment of police officers," he said.

Willis Caruso, the housing authority's general counsel, contended that the Constitution allows warrantless searches as long as the methods do not violate the Fourth Amendment's prohibition against "unreasonable searches and seizures."

14 GANGS, GUNS, AND VIOLENCE

GANGS WITH A VISION OF PEACE

Lee Ranck

Lee Ranck is a staff writer for Christian Social Action, *a journal on social affairs published by the United Methodist Church.*

Points to Consider:

1. Describe the Gang Summit in Kansas City.

2. What were the four goals of the Summit organizers?

3. Identify a gang stereotype.

4. Explain any actions that could improve poor city neighborhoods.

Lee Ranck, "Gangs with a Vision of Peace," **Christian Social Action**, June 1993.

"I will do whatever it takes to feed my children."

Describing this emotional conclusion to the 1993 National Urban Peace and Justice Summit, which met in Kansas City, Missouri, Jerald Scott, staff member of the General Board of Church and Society, said: "I'll never be the same after this experience, and I am committed to see that the movement that they are trying to start doesn't stop."

Scott, who was recently named national coordinator for the United Methodism's Special Program on Substance Abuse and Related Violence, was invited to participate in the summit as an official observer because of her "continuing work towards the reclaiming of urban America." United Methodist Bishop Felton E. May, who headed the bishops' initiative on drugs and drug violence, was also invited as an official observer.

Some 100 leaders of urban gangs, mostly African American and Hispanic American, from 20 US cities participated in the event, first dubbed "Gang Summit," then renamed to emphasize the positive and productive meeting. In addition, some 40 mostly non-white adults, among them Scott, participated as advisors and observers. The summit was dedicated to the memory of Cesar Chavez.

The summit grew out of the truce in Los Angeles, following the riots after the Rodney King verdict, between the Crips and the Bloods. It aimed at bringing together gang leaders seeking to end urban violence and to rebuild their local communities. Summit prime mover was Carl Upchurch, national coordinator of The Council for Urban Peace and Justice, headquartered in Granville, Ohio...

DIALOGUE TO IDENTIFY ISSUES

The National Urban Peace and Justice Summit was designed, its mission statement said, to "bring together individuals who have been affected by gangs from communities throughout the United States in a safe environment for the purpose of beginning a dialogue to identify common issues and potential solutions. This gathering is only a beginning. Information shared at the summit will be taken by participants and observers back into their own communities for continuing dialogue and work. Communities must make a commitment to continue the dialogue and work towards solutions."

Cartoon by Mike Ramirez. Reprinted with permission of **Coply News Service**.

"The goal," the mission statement continued, "is providing individuals who choose to put aside gang affiliations, for the purpose of eliciting a firm commitment to nonviolent change, a forum to begin the process of communication." Summit organizers set four principal issue areas for discussion:

1. Recognizing and supporting leadership in the United States that is originating in the streets.

2. Developing a new vision for US cities; finding practical approaches to sustain the gang truce; identifying and isolating obstacles to peace; understanding the historical issues underlying the present situation.

3. Obtaining economic justice in urban United States; effecting and facilitating alternative economic development plans.

4. Addressing police abuse and brutality and finding alternative responses to such actions.

These issue areas became the focus of four "breakout" sessions in which gang members participated with the observers. (Scott, for instance, was part of the "new visions" discussion.) The Rev. Benjamin Chavis, recently appointed NAACP executive director, and Dr. Jean Sindab, with the NCC Prophetic Justice Unit, served as co-chairs of the Observer Advisory Council.

SHATTERING THE SOCIAL MISFIT STEREOTYPE

"This summit has demystified who gang members are and shattered the stereotype that they are some social misfits," Chavis told *Washington Post* reporter Gary Lee. "We have to involve the victims of inner-city neglect in helping us find solutions to it. We see this summit as only the beginning."

GBCS staffer Scott was among those who experienced that demystification. She said, "I was apprehensive when I first went because I didn't know what to expect. I got there feeling like I was the social activist who was going to help change things, and then I realized how out of touch, even as an African American woman, I had been with people whose daily lives I just cannot even imagine. I wondered what it would mean to have to live in that kind of a violent environment every day. And yet, they are no different from me; they want the same things I want."

One young man told Scott, "I will do whatever it takes to feed my children." "I'd feel the same way if I had kids," she responded. "The more I was around these young folks and listened to the terribly violent things they had to do to survive, I understood that circumstances are making them live that way, even though they don't want to. Therefore, Scott said, "we began to talk about ways to move their illegal work habits to work styles that are legal."

Scott, who has for several years been the front person working on drug and alcohol concerns for the General Board of Church and Society, said that the issue of drug and drug use really didn't come up at the summit, except in terms of an economic means of support. The discussions, she said, centered on "empowerment and getting themselves together economically, changing their lifestyles from violent, illegal behavior to peaceful, legal work so they could function in society."

TO IMPROVE INNER-CITY NEIGHBORHOODS

At the summit's end, organizers indicated they would work to increase the number of gang truces across the nation. They also recommended a number of actions to improve inner-city neighborhoods. These included:

> # RIOTS
>
> *After riots in Los Angeles, leaders of street gangs there and in several other cities, including Minneapolis, called truces. The truces have helped reduce gang-related shootings in those communities. So, in a move to encourage more peace treaties, 120 gang leaders from 22 cities are planning to meet today in Kansas City, Mo., for a three-day summit.*
>
> Alex Kotlowitz, "A Truce in Gang Wars Yields Mixed Results, Minneapolis Discovers," **The Wall Street Journal**, April 29, 1993.

- broadening the national service programs;

- creating citizen patrols with video cameras to document cases of police brutality;

- setting up a national commission of minority group members to probe brutality reports;

- initiating economic development programs;

- establishing (by the Clinton administration) 500,000 jobs for at-risk youth.

President Clinton, in fact, spoke to the summit participants when asked during a newspaper interview whether he had a message for the gang members meeting in Kansas City. "There's a better way to live, and I'm doing my best to create more opportunities for you," the President said. "You have to decide what kind of life you want to live, and whether you want to have a long life, and whether you want it to be full of conflict and danger or whether you want to be able to make something of your life and have it come out differently."

"This was a very positive experience, no matter how it got reported in the media," Scott concluded. "They discussed how they could best serve their communities and make them a positive place rather than a negative place in which to live."

"I came away feeling more strongly than ever about the effective policy statements we have as The United Methodist Church that really speak to the systematic issues that make a person into someone who doesn't care about anything because of the oppression he or she suffers with the poverty and violence and drugs."

15 GANGS, GUNS, AND VIOLENCE

WE MUST PROSECUTE GANG CRIMINAL VIOLENCE

Orin Hatch

Orin Hatch is a United States Republican Senator from Utah and a prominent conservative leader in Congress.

Points to Consider:

1. Explain the meaning of "The Project."

2. How is the "Dole-Hatch Amendment" defined?

3. What is the first responsibility of government?

4. How should the federal government be involved in the prevention of crime?

Excerpted from a Senate speech by Orin Hatch, November 8, 1993.

*The first responsibility of government is to ensure the
safety of the public.*

Our nation is currently witnessing an unprecedented growth in
gang violence, a scourge all too well known to cities like Los
Angeles and New York City. What used to be a problem of our
nation's largest cities, gangs have invaded the cities like Wichita,
KS, and Salt Lake City, in my own home state.

The problem of gang and youth violence is a great concern to
the citizens of my state. According to the Salt Lake Area Gang
Project, a multijurisdictional task force created in 1989 to fight
gang crime in the Salt Lake area, there are at least 215 identified
gangs in our region with over 1,700 members. That is hard to
believe, but it is true.

GANGS AND VIOLENCE

The Project informs me that gang-related crime incidents have
risen from 388 in 1991 to over 3,100 in the first 7 months of this
year. While many of these offenses are property crimes, I have to
say assaults and shootings continue to grow as well. In fact, there
were over 62 drive-by shootings and 3 homicides attributable to
gang violence in Utah in the first 7 months of this year.

Juvenile involvement in Utah's gangs is substantial, accounting
for 34 percent of gang membership, and members usually range
from 15 to 22 years of age. The young people of our inner cities
need to be steered away from gang involvement. As well, law
enforcement needs tools to intervene early in the lives of these
troubled minors. Gang intervention efforts are critical to the Salt
Lake Valley, the entire State of Utah and, frankly, to every State of
the Union. That is why we need to ensure continued funding for
projects like the Salt Lake Area Gang Project.

THE PROJECT

The Project has worked to interdict gang activity, mobilize communities, and provide gang intelligence to police agencies. Salt
Lake City, Sandy City, Murray City, and other surrounding cities
all contribute manpower to this effort. The Hatch-Dole amendment ensures continued funding for this project. Recently, the
Senate passed legislation similar to this aspect of the Hatch-Dole
amendment. Funding for multijurisdictional gang task forces must
be passed so that our struggling cities are provided the funds nec-

BOB ROGERS reprinted with permission of **UFS, Inc.**

essary to combat gang and youth violence.

The Hatch-Dole, or Dole-Hatch, gang amendment also incorporates many other aspects of the Dole-Hatch crime bill. It includes a provision providing for the powerful arm of the federal government to be made available to state and local law enforcement agencies to help combat gang violence.

The amendment makes it a federal offense to engage in gang-related crime and subjects gang members to stiff mandatory minimum penalties. For example, gang members who recruit others into criminal gangs or engage in criminal conduct shall be subject to a mandatory minimum penalty of 5 years imprisonment. If a gang offense involves attempted murder, the perpetrator faces a mandatory minimum sentence of 20 years imprisonment, and if there is murder, the gang member faces a possible death sentence.

PROSECUTION

Criminal gang leaders who use juveniles in criminal enterprises for financial gain will be subject to the same penalties as organized crime leaders. That is important. It is tough. It is going to mean something, and it is going to make people think twice before they involve our teenagers in these crimes.

Our amendment also provides for adult prosecution of serious juvenile offenders, increased penalties for employing children to distribute drugs near schools or playgrounds or public housing and for travel act crimes involving violence and conspiracy to commit contractual killings. As well, our amendment provides $50 million for additional federal prosecutors who will be assigned to fight gang violence. These additional prosecutors will make implementation of this gang measure a reality by ensuring that additional prosecutors will be assigned to cities where most needed.

GRANTS

Finally, the Hatch-Dole amendment establishes a $100 million grant program for efforts at the state and local level, and by private not-for-profit anticrime organizations to assist in prevention and enforcement programs aimed at fighting juvenile gangs. Funding formulated under this provision will be allocated to each of the states as follows: Each state would receive a minimum of $500,000, or 1 percent, whichever is greater, and the balance would be distributed to each state based on a ratio of the population of juveniles residing in the state as compared to the population of juveniles residing in the country.

PUBLIC SAFETY

The first responsibility of government is to ensure the safety of the public. It is true that state and local governments now handle over 95 percent of the criminal cases filed each year. The crime bill we are debating recognizes this fact by proposing a significant increase in financial assistance to states to hire additional police, build more prisons and jails, and make schools safer. I submit, however, that the federal government's role in assisting the states' fight against violent crime must be measured by more than financial support.

The federal government, as a result of the Controlled Substance Act, has jurisdiction over virtually all drug trafficking, manufacturing, and distribution offenses. Yet, most drug cases are still prosecuted at the state and local level. This is because the federal law enforcement agencies have worked in a cooperative manner with local officials so that the U.S. resources can be used most effectively. I am unaware of a single state or local prosecutor who opposes the federal government's assistance in these cases.

FEDERAL ASSISTANCE

The Hatch-Dole anti-gang amendment does not transfer the exclusive jurisdiction of gang offenses from the states to the federal government. Rather, it permits the federal government to assist the states in their ongoing effort to fight gang violence. This amendment does not relieve the states of any responsibility for prosecuting gangs or other violent crime. It simply permits federal assistance.

Some of my colleagues have little or no trouble proposing that we federalize the delivery and payment of health care services, labor/management relations, teacher standards, energy policy, environmental standards, child support collection, reproductive rights, and other issues too numerous to list. Yet, when the issue before the Congress is the safety of law-abiding Americans, oftentimes the enthusiasm for federal intervention dissipates. Their position is understandable. After all, if federal resources must be devoted to fighting crime, there may be less resources available to address their particular interests. In my view, however, Congress should not get into these additional areas until our principal obligation to the American people has been met.

FEDERAL CASES

The Senator from Delaware and I differ somewhat on this amendment, but he is not opposed to federalizing all criminal matters. The Senate adopted an amendment to this bill authored by our chairman which federalizes crimes motivated by gender. I am a cosponsor of this measure and worked with our distinguished friend, Senator Biden, to pass it.

I appreciate the fact that federal judges are opposed to the increasing trend toward federalizing crimes. Yet, claims that criminal cases are taking up a disproportionate amount of federal filings are not supported by the facts. According to the Administrative Office of the U.S. Courts, the criminal caseload per judge is nearly 50 percent below that of 1972. The number of criminal cases reached a 40-year peak in 1972, and despite all of the cries from the defense bar, the number of criminal cases filed in 1992 was actually 14 percent below the 1972 figure. There were less criminal cases in federal courts in 1992 than there were in 1972, even though the number of authorized judges is now 62 percent higher than in 1972.

Mr. President, the choice is clear. If my colleagues truly want to provide the states the assistance they need in fighting gang violence, both financial support and jurisdictional support, then they should support this amendment, and I hope they will.

16   GANGS, GUNS, AND VIOLENCE

A SPIRITUAL PLAN TO SAVE URBAN AMERICA

Jim Wallis and the Boston Churches

Jim Wallis is the editor and founder of Sojourners *magazine. The ten-point program that follows the article by Jim Wallis was drafted by churches working in Boston's inner city neighborhoods.*

Points to Consider:

1. How serious is the problem of violence in America?

2. How are spiritual concerns related to the problem of violence?

3. What role can the churches play?

4. Explain the 10 point plan by Boston churches to deal with youth violence.

Jim Wallis, "The Churches Mobilize to Save Urban America," **Sojourners**, February/March 1994, Reprinted with permission from **Sojourners**, 2401 15th St. NW, Washington, DC, 20009, (202) 328-8842.

"Black children are drowning in their own blood on the streets...and the church has that blood on its hands."

Boston. A young man fleeing two pursuers with automatic weapons ducks into a church during a worship service, believing he will be safe there. His assailants don't even pause at the church door as they rush in and open fire. The choir stops singing, the preacher dives under the pulpit, and the congregation crouches beneath the pews as the sanctuary is sprayed with bullets.

Later, at a press conference, church leaders indignantly decry the blasphemous violation of holy thresholds and sacred space. But Azusa Christian Community's Eugene Rivers, an African-American street pastor, offered a different and prophetic word: "If the church won't go into the streets, the streets will come into the church."

Washington, DC All the Sunday morning talk shows focus on out-of-control violence in the United States. Nobody is safe, says a worried-looking David Brinkley. Desperate politicians and police chiefs talk crime bills and gun registrations and the President speaks of the breakdown of work, family, and community. What's most clear is that the political and media elites haven't got a clue as to what to do. Sunday night, the children living in the capital of the world's last remaining superpower go to bed to the sound of gunfire.

Palestine, Eighth-Century B.C.E. The prophet Isaiah delivers oracles to the children of Israel and to the neighboring Egyptians about the plight of their societies:

Their land is filled with silver and gold, and there is no end to their treasures; their land is filled with horses, and there is no end to their chariots. Their land is filled with idols; they bow down to the work of their hands, to what their fingers have made. And so the people are humbled; and everyone is brought low.

The consequence, the prophet continues, of a society's greed, social injustice, and idol worship is judgment in the form of spiritual degradation, violence, and the break-up of community. The people turn on one another; "they will fight, one against the other, neighbor against neighbor, city against city, kingdom against kingdom." The people's "spirit" will be "emptied out" (Isaiah 2 and 19).

Cartoon by Joe Heller.

I WILL NEVER FORGET a conversation with some young Crips and Bloods in Watts after the Los Angeles eruption. When asked what the churches could do to help, an 18-year-old gang member looked us straight in the eyes and said: "We need the churches to lead us to the Lord." I now believe that in responding to this call the churches themselves will be led back to the Lord.

The escalation of violence on our nation's streets has reached such a crisis that perhaps only the religious community can adequately respond to it. Why? Because the cruel and endemic economic injustice, soul-killing materialism, life-destroying drug traffic, pervasive racism, unprecedented breakdown of family life and structure, and almost total collapse of moral values that have created this culture of violence are, at heart, spiritual issues.

The frightening disregard for human life among too many young people is a bitter reflection of the way these same young people have become so utterly disregarded by their society. The coldness of heart that now makes even veteran urban activists shiver is a judgment upon our coldness toward our poorest children. We reap what we have sown.

Neither liberal sociology nor conservative piety can begin to address the roots of this crisis. Neither government spending nor simplistic self-help slogans will suffice. What is called for now is that particular biblical combination of which the prophets most often joke – justice and righteousness. Both the structures of oppression and the morality of personal behavior must undergo radical transformation. We need a change of heart and a change of direction not only among troubled urban youth, but for all of us.

BECAUSE SPIRITUAL transformation will be at the absolute core of the changes we so urgently need, the churches must help lead the way. But such a leadership role will first require some soul-searching on the part of the churches. At the recent National Congress of Black Churches' Consultation on Violence and Our Youth, in New Orleans, it was painfully acknowledged that "black children are drowning in their own blood on the streets...and the church has that blood on its hands."

This problem is too deep and our task too large to take it on by ourselves. We will need the help that comes "by faith." As another young man in that post-riot meeting in Watts said to us, "We've got some habits that only God can cure." That goes for all of us.

The contribution of faith communities to a social crisis always comes precisely at the point of perceived lost causes and hopeless circumstances. The writer of the Letter to the Hebrews says that "faith is the substance of things hoped for, the evidence of things not seen" (11:1). Or, as I like to paraphrase it, hope is believing in spite of the evidence, then watching the evidence change. At critical historical junctures, faith makes possible the political imagination to find solutions to seemingly impossible social problems. Hopeful signs are already apparent.

10 POINT PLAN

This plan emerged from churches working in Boston's inner-city neighborhoods. The following 10 point proposal for citywide church mobilization is born of the realities of our day-to-day work with the youth on the streets, in the crack houses, and in the courts and jails of this city. We seek to generate serious discussion regarding the specific ways the Christian community can bring the peace of God to the violent world of our youth. We therefore call upon churches, church agencies, and the academic theological community throughout the city to consider, discuss, debate, and implement, singly or in collaboration, any one or more of the following proposals:

100

SHADOW OF SLAVERY

*More than 10 million black people now face a crisis of cata-
strophic proportions. Life in American inner-cities is poor,
brutish, and short; and future prospects are even bleaker.*

*Unlike many of our ancestors, who came out of slavery and
entered this century with strong backs, discipline, a thirst for
literacy, deep religious faith, and hope born of that faith, we
have produced a generation that does not "know the ways of
the Lord"—a "new jack" generation ill-equipped to secure
gainful employment even as productive slaves. This generation provides unique insight into current economic opportunities.*

*Consider this achievement: A generation of poor black
men, women, and children may reach the end of this century
in a position worse than their ancestors who entered the century in the shadow of slavery. Unable to see a more rational
future through the eyes of faith, they lack the hope that sustained their forebears. Lacking hope, they experience what
sociologist Orlando Patterson has called "social death." But
unlike the social death of slavery, this new social death is fun-
damentally spiritual. Rooted in the destruction of faith and
hope, it produces a world in which history and identity are
themselves divested of meaning, a world of nihilism and
despair.*

Eugene F. Rivers, "Take Your Inheritance," **Sojourners**, February/March, 1994.

1. To establish four or five church cluster-collaborations that
sponsor "Adopt a Gang" programs to organize and evangelize
youth in gangs. Inner-city churches would serve as drop-in centers providing sanctuary for troubled youth.

2. To commission missionaries to serve as advocates for black
and Latino juveniles in the courts. Such missionaries would work
closely with probation officers, law enforcement officials, and
youth street workers to assist at-risk youth and their families. To
convene summit meetings between school superintendents, principals of public middle and high schools, and black and Latino
pastors to develop partnerships that will focus on the youth most
at risk. We propose to do pastoral work with the most violent and

troubled young people and their families. In our judgment, this is a rational alternative to ill-conceived proposals to suspend the principle of due process.

3. To commission youth evangelists to do street-level one-on-one evangelism with youth involved in drug trafficking. These evangelists would also work to prepare these youth for participation in the economic life of the nation. Such work might include preparation for college, the development of legal revenue-generating enterprises, and the acquisition of trade skills and union membership.

4. To establish accountable community-based economic development projects that go beyond "market and state" visions of revenue generation. Such economic development initiatives will include community land trusts, micro-enterprise projects, worker cooperatives, community finance institutions, consumer cooperatives, and democratically run community development corporations.

5. To establish links between suburban and downtown churches and front-line ministries to provide spiritual, human resource, and material support.

6. To initiate and support neighborhood crime-watch programs within local church neighborhoods. If, for example, 200 churches covered the four corners surrounding their sites, 800 blocks would be safer.

7. To establish working relationships between local churches and community-based health centers to provide pastoral counseling for families during times of crisis. We also propose the initiation of abstinence-oriented educational programs focusing on the prevention of AIDS and sexually transmitted diseases.

8. To convene a working summit meeting for Christian black and Latino men in order to discuss the development of Christian brotherhoods that would provide rational alternatives to violent gang life. Such brotherhoods would also be charged with fostering responsibility to family and protecting houses of worship.

9. To establish rape crisis drop-in centers and services for battered women in churches. Counseling programs must be established for abusive men, particularly teen-agers and young adults.

10. To develop an aggressive black and Latino history curricu-

lum, with an additional focus on the struggles of women and poor people. Such a curriculum could be taught in churches as a means of helping our youth to understand that the God of history has been and remains active in the lives of all peoples.

Principal authors: Jeffrey L. Brown, Union Baptist Church; Ray A. Hammond, Bethel African Methodist Episcopal Church; Eugene F. Rivers, Azusa Christian Community; Susie Thomas, Mt. Olive Temple of Christ; Gilbert A. Thompson, New Covenant Christian Center; Bruce H. Wall, Dorchester Temple Baptist Church; Samuel C. Wood, Lord's Family African Methodist Episcopal Zion Church. Brown, Hammond, and Wood are members of the executive committee of the Ten Point Coalition.

RECOGNIZING AUTHOR'S POINT OF VIEW

This activity may be used as an individualized study guide for students in libraries and resource centers or as a discussion catalyst in small group and classroom discussions.

Guidelines

Good readers make clear distinctions between descriptive articles that relate factual information and articles that express a point of view. Articles that express editorial commentary and analysis are featured in this publication. Examine the following statements. Then try to decide if any of these statements take a similar position to any of the authors in Chapter Three. Working as individuals or in small groups, try to match the point of view in each statement below with the most appropriate reading in Chapter Three. Mark the appropriate reading number in front of each statement. Mark (O) for any statement that cannot be associated with the point of view of any reading in Chapter Three.

_____ 1. Gang recruits can most often be classified as desperate, otherwise they would not risk their lives for so little return.

_____ 2. The "war on drugs" or "war on gangs" often translates into a war on people of color.

_____ 3. The Judeo-Christian Community must mobilize their synagogues and churches to aid in the underlying problems of poverty and abuse to solve the problem of adolescent violence.

_____4. Curbing gang violence requires tough legislation and penalties for youth offenders committing violent crimes. Many of these crimes need to be addressed by federal law.

_____5. Parental accountability is key in solving the youth violence dilemma.

_____6. Meetings like the Gang Summit in Kansas City (1993) should be encouraged rather than shunned.

_____7. The "epidemic" of youth violence has been grossly overblown.

_____8. The blood must stop being shed before anyone can focus on urban reformation and economic prosperity.

_____9. The breakdown of the family unit is a root cause of adolescent crime.

_____10. Rural areas should not be ignored as areas with problems of adolescent crime and drug abuse. They should also obtain federal target monies to combat these problems.

CHAPTER 4

PREVENTING YOUTH VIOLENCE

17 PREVENTING YOUTH VIOLENCE

GUN LAWS WILL CURB VIOLENCE

Marian Wright Edelman

Marian Wright Edelman is president of the Children's Defense Fund in Washington, DC.

Points to Consider:

1. How serious is gun-related violence in the U.S.?

2. Compare the extent of U.S. gun-related violence to that of other nations.

3. Summarize the problem of gun-related violence among black youth.

4. Why are schools referred to as war zones?

5. What will getting rid of guns accomplish?

Excerpted from testimony by Marian Wright Edelman before the Select Committee on Children, Youth, and Families, March 10, 1993.

Prison walls are bulging with the 1.1 million inmates that make us the world's leading jailor.

Gun-related violence takes the life of an American child at least every 3 hours and the lives of at least 25 children–the equivalent of a classroomful–every 3 days. In 1990 alone, guns were used to kill 222 children under the age of 10, and 6,795 adolescents, teenagers, and young adults under the age of 25. Besides the children killed by guns, the National Education Association reports that about another 30 children are injured every day by guns. The Harlem Hospital in New York has found that the majority of children admitted with gunshot wounds already have lost a family member to a fatal, gun-related injury.

Since 1988, teenage boys in the United States generally have been more likely to die from gunshot wounds than from all natural causes combined, according to the National Center for Health Statistics. And, in a mere 3 years–between 1987 and 1990–gunshot wounds among children ages 16 and under in urban areas nearly doubled, according to the National Pediatric Trauma Registry.

SENSELESS KILLING

Nothing more graphically illustrates the moral tumor growing on the American soul than our acquiescence in this senseless killing of innocent children. No other industrialized nation even approaches the United States' incidence of firearms-related violence. According to the Center to Prevent Handgun Violence, in 1990, handguns were used to murder 13 people in Sweden, 91 people in Switzerland, 87 people in Japan, 68 people in Canada, 22 people in Great Britain, and 10 people in Australia. By comparison, handguns were used to murder 10,567 people in the United States. And, even handguns cannot kill or injure fast enough for the nearly 1 million private owners of semi-automatic weapons.

The deadly combination of guns, gangs, drugs, poverty, and traumatized and hopeless youths is turning many of our inner-cities into zones of destruction and despair and our neighborhoods and schools into corridors of fear. For thousands of inner-city youths, the American dream has become a choice between prison and death. In fact, prison has become a more positive option than home and neighborhood for many youths who see no hope, no safety, no jobs, and no future outside prison walls. A Latino youth told a CNN reporter that he just hoped he could grow up and "go to prison and not be dead."

BLACK YOUTH

Homicide is the leading cause of death among black youths ages 18 to 24. According to the Centers for Disease Control, between 1984 and 1988, the murder rate of black youths between the ages of 15 and 19 rose by 100 percent. And, a study in *The New England Journal of Medicine* found that young men in Harlem are less likely to live to age 40 than their counterparts in Bangladesh.

However, it is not just poor or black children who are at risk today. Nor is it just children in the large inner-cities. Countless affluent and middle-income white and brown and Asian-American children, like their poor and minority counterparts, are so adrift that they turn to drugs and alcohol, as well as to the violence we market incessantly to them. Just recently, *The New York Times* has published two separate articles on gang-related violence in communities we normally might consider safe havens: Little Rock, AK and Wichita, KS, as well as even smaller communities in Kansas. Garden City, a western Kansas community of only 24,000, has 7 gangs, at least one of which was running a crack house. Johnson County, an affluent Kansas City suburb, has 16 identified gangs, with at least several hundred members.

WAR ZONES

Our schools have become zones of fear and danger instead of places of excitement and nurturing and genuine learning. During a single 6 month period in 1988-89, more than 400,000 students were victims of violent crime at school. A 1990 survey of students at 31 Illinois high schools revealed that one in 20 students had carried a gun to school. California schools reported a 200-percent increase in gun confiscations from students between 1986 and 1990. In a 1987 survey of high school students, 48 percent of tenth-grade boys and 34 percent of eighth-grade boys said they could get a handgun if they wanted one.

In New York City, arrests on gun charges of youngsters ages 10 to 15 increased by 75 percent between 1987 and 1990. Astonishingly, a recent Northeastern University study found that arrests for murder of boys 12 years of age and under doubled between 1985 and 1991.

Our urban and suburban war zones are, unsurprisingly, a real-life reflection of the American worship of violence, which has become a leading national pastime and prime-time obsession. Violent acts are the daily fare of millions of children who watch TV an average of 21 hours per week. *TV Guide* reports a violent incident is shown, on average, every 6 minutes.

While we wait for community-based, church-based, and school-based violence-prevention programs to curb the incidence of violence, and while we work for and wait for investment programs to give new hope and opportunity to America's children, we must work–and not wait–to reduce the lethality of violence.

GET RID OF GUNS

There is only one way to do that–by getting guns off our streets, and out of our schools, and out of our homes. As President Clinton said, "[not] everybody in America needs to be able to buy a semi-automatic or an automatic weapon, built only for the purpose of killing people, in order to protect the right of Americans to hunt and practice marksmanship and to be secure." Disarming Americans is a public-health emergency, similar to a resurgence of smallpox or plague. We know how to inoculate ourselves; we just have to do it.

This is not a matter of civil liberties. Nor is it a matter of criminal justice. This is a matter of public health. Prison walls are bulging with the 1.1 million inmates that make us the world's leading jailor. Yet violence continues to escalate along with prison costs. All our jails cannot protect us against injustice.

In order to address the root causes of our Nation's epidemic of violence, we must work to implement the programs that we know will help protect children from violence. First, it is absolutely essential that Congress pass legislation to fund fully the Head Start program and once again pass the Child Welfare and Family Preservation Act, which President Bush vetoed as part of the urban aid/tax bill. Head Start offers children and families comprehensive services and a safe haven while assuring that children enter school ready to learn. The Child Welfare and Family Preservation provisions are designed to help families nurture, protect, and support better their children and assure quality out-of-home care for those children who cannot be protected at home.

Second, I urge you and Congress to pass—and fund—the Family Investment Act and the Job Training Reform Amendments, as well as the community policing bill that Senator Dodd intends to introduce. Only with these kinds of measures will we fulfill our obligation to provide our children with positive, constructive, and nurturing alternatives to violence.

GUN LAWS

Third, I urge you to pass all the currently pending gun control legislation, namely, the Brady bill, the Federal Firearm Licensing Act, the Gun Theft Act, the Bullet Death, Injury, and Family Dissolution Control Act, the Multiple Handgun Transfer Prohibition Act of 1993, and the Strict Liability for Safer Streets Act.

In addition, Representative Serrano introduced the Classroom Safety Act, which would provide $100 million a year in federal grants to help local school districts develop and implement programs to prevent violence. Among others, these could include service programs for school staff, conflict resolution training for students, and drug-prevention or anti-gang efforts. I urge you to pass that bill as well.

111

18   PREVENTING YOUTH VIOLENCE

GUN LAWS WILL NOT CURB VIOLENCE

Susan R. Lamson

Susan R. Lamson made the following statement as Director of the Federal Affairs Division of the National Rifle Association of America's Institute for Legislative Action.

Points to Consider:

1. How widespread are firearms-related deaths and injuries?

2. What can be done to prevent firearms-related accidents?

3. How is television related to violence in the streets?

4. Identify the causes of school violence.

5. Why does the author oppose gun laws?

Excerpted from testimony by Susan R. Lamson before the Subcommittee on Juvenile Justice of the Senate Committee on the Judiciary, June 9 and September 13, 1993.

Youth violence is no more a product of lax, or a lack of, gun laws than is similar adult violence.

It may be trite to state, but it is no less true, that our young people are our future. The subject we address today involves at least three different components: the lawful use of firearms by young people; firearms as a real or potential threat to young people because of accidents; and the abuse and misuse of firearms in crime by young people.

MOTIVATIONS

Obviously, it is the third part of this problem which must be examined. This issue relates to the motivations of young people who carry firearms and commit crimes, and the failure of the criminal justice system to recognize and address the scope of this problem. It appears that society's failure to deal with crime in a meaningful way, embodied in our "catch and release" criminal justice system, begins with and has its most deleterious effects on our youth.

SAFETY

Although this subcommittee is not addressing the lawful use of firearms by millions of young people, the value of firearms training as a recreational pursuit should not be overlooked. At the present time, firearms-related deaths are the fourth leading cause of childhood deaths and account for 3 percent of all accidental deaths of children aged 0-14. This is hardly insignificant, but relative to the risk of drowning, fires, or auto accidents, the risk is considerably less. For instance, a child is 13 times more likely to die in an auto accident, and more than four times as likely to die in a fire or be drowned.

The NRA is the recognized leader in providing safe firearms handling and instruction to both young and old alike. We believe wholeheartedly that firearms training is a lifesaver, and that it is a message that everyone should hear. Our "Eddie Eagle" firearms safety training program, based on a cartoon character of the same name, is geared toward small children. This program has been given out to literally millions of individuals, schools, and community organizations and is specifically designed to instill in young children one idea—that guns are dangerous and should be avoided.

RESPONSIBILITY

Responsibility remains the key in preventing firearms-related accidents. A firearm, loaded or otherwise, does not belong within a small child's sphere of influence. Irresponsible behavior by adults which allows children unsupervised access to firearms is no accident, nor can it be legislated away.

However, it is one thing to teach a child that a firearm should never be pointed in a unsafe direction, yet quite another to instill in that child the values which engender respect for human life. The criminal misuse of firearms is a manifestation of a deeper societal dysfunction which goes to less tractable problems that cannot be addressed by a message delivered by cartoon characters. To name but one factor, the effects of exposure to violence, particularly as it relates to television exposure during the impressionable years, is finally beginning to gain recognition as a serious problem.

The NRA recently submitted testimony to Congress concerning our suggestions for developing standards to limit the impact of media influences on young people. Our recommendations are predicated on the assumption that those who control the media are responsible participants in this debate, and should be willing to take voluntary steps to limit the unintentional exposure of young minds to gratuitous violence.

We know from experience that teaching young people to respect firearms has to be balanced against numerous competing, and often conflicting, influences. For instance, we know that careless handling of a firearm by a popular movie or television program neutralizes the message we are trying to convey. However, what happens when the message is that violence is a means to an end? That is the problem this subcommittee is confronting.

MORAL VALUES

What sadder commentary can there be on the failure to instill moral values and respect for the sanctity of human life in our youth when, over the last decade, violent crime by juveniles has more than doubled in the United States. In 1982 there was a murder committed by a juvenile approximately every 40 days. In 1992, a murder was committed by a juvenile every 12 days. In 1982, a juvenile committed a rape every 26 days; by 1992 it was every 8 days. The statistics on violent behavior may partially include every race and income group, but those who ignore the fact that there is a overwhelmingly disproportionate impact on poor, black and Hispanic inner-city youths are not focusing on where the problem lies.

The pathologies of the inner-city cannot be remedied by creating stronger laws, unless of course we can pass laws that every family has two caring parents; unless we can pass laws that reverse the pernicious effects of drugs and widespread alcohol use in our inner-cities; unless we can pass laws outlawing poverty; unless we can pass laws that give young people stability and the knowledge that they can reach their goals by hard work and perseverance–and that the goals are worth reaching.

Last year, Professors Joseph Sheley, Zina McGee and James Wright published "Gun-Related Violence in and Around Inner-City Schools"–the results of a cross-sectional survey of ten inner-city high schools in several states. Noting that "nearly everything that leads to gun-related violence among youths is already against the law," the researchers' prescription was neither more gun restrictions, metal detectors, nor shake-downs of students, but "a concerted effort to rebuild the social structure of inner-cities."

VIOLENCE

Sheley, McGee and Wright found that violence in our schools does not spring from the classroom floor: "Rather, violence spills into the schools from the world outside....Structurally, we are experiencing the development of an inner-city underclass unlike any in our past. In a shrinking industrial economy, we are witnessing the disintegration of the traditional family, increasing poverty and homelessness, diminishing health, and deteriorating educational institutions."

It is interesting to consider why, when we read the statistics on the number of assaults, rapes, robberies and murders that occur in our schools, we question how it is that our children feel obligated to provide for their own protection. I ask you, would any member of this committee feel safe under similar circumstances? It appears to be no less true that one of the primary reasons why many young people are bringing guns to school is because they believe they need to do so. Until we can reverse this belief in fact, it is doubtful that many students are going to accept it in theory. To the extent that this can be accomplished by limiting the factors that allow youthful criminals to acquire the means to commit these acts, we support such measures.

SOLUTIONS

The unfortunate conclusion to my testimony is that there are no easy solutions to this problem, only hard realities. The hard reality is that we have a long and a short-term problem. The long-term problem is that we have raised a generation of which far too many of its members are loathe to recognize any moral authority, or community boundary. Until we are willing and able to address the underlying failings that have led us to this juncture, this problem is only going to worsen. The short-term problem is that we have far too many children who fit the chronological definition, but are adults by behavior.

In this vein, youth violence is no more a product of lax, or a lack of, gun laws than is similar adult violence. No amount of regulation, up to and including a total ban on all firearms use by minors, will have any significant effect on the level of juvenile violent crime, until we begin to get serious about enforcing existing laws and incarcerating law breakers.

The preservation of order in our society is directly related to a functioning, effective system of protection for the rights of Americans and prosecution of those who abuse those rights. Our democracy cannot survive without these protections. The NRA intends to do its part and we are willing to work with any Member of Congress to craft proposals which will help to achieve criminal justice reform.

116

PROTECTING PUBLIC SAFETY

Robert K. Corbin

From 1979 to 1990 Robert K. Corbin was Attorney General for the State of Arizona. He wrote this article as the president of the National Rifle Association.

Points to Consider:

1. What is wrong with the juvenile courts?

2. Summarize any actions that might prevent juvenile crime and violence.

3. Describe the reform proposals for the juvenile justice system.

4. How is public housing related to youth crime?

Excerpted from Congressional testimony by Robert K. Corbin before the Subcommittee on Juvenile Justice of the Senate Committee on the Judiciary, June 1 and 2, 1993.

117

Sadly, the juvenile justice system is a blunt instrument. It only restores order through force.

Nowhere are the problems of endemic violence and the failure to address these problems more keenly felt than in our juvenile justice system–and the magnitude of the problem is startling. What sadder commentary can there be on the failure to instill moral values and respect for the sanctity of human life in our youth when, as just one example, over the last decade, violent crime by juveniles in this country has more than doubled. In 1982 there was a murder committed by a juvenile approximately every 40 days. In 1992 a murder was committed by a juvenile every 12 days. In 1982 a juvenile committed a rape every 26 days; by 1992 it was every 8 days.

The discussion in which you engage today is much more than a discussion over numbers and trends and calculations. It is about lives broken by juvenile violence and by the government's failure to discharge its most sacred promise to the people; to secure domestic tranquility and to protect life, liberty, and property. Behind each one of these statistics is the story of a victim; a lost or shattered life, a devastated family, and all too often a story of yet another collapse of our justice system.

JUVENILE COURTS

By the weakness of our juvenile courts, we are encouraging the very conduct they are established to deter. Just as the Congress in recent years has recognized the need to discipline the federal courts' sentencing policies through the guidelines and use of mandatory sentences for chronic and violent offenders, so, too, must the juvenile courts of this country be disciplined by mandated transfer laws. And for the cases they continue to hear, there must be tough-minded, graduated sanctions which emphasize consequences and responsibility for younger, non-violent first time offenders.

Juvenile justice reform must be a key element in this country's strategy to control and reduce the violent crime which ravages our citizens. The NRA supports reasonable regulations on the carrying of firearms by juveniles. Those who believe otherwise are ignorant of the reforms we have promoted to deal with this issue. No one should be fooled into believing that any amount of regulation, up to and including a total ban on all firearms use by minors,

STEVE BENSON reprinted with permission of **UFS, Inc.**

will have any effect on the level of juvenile violent crime. All such measures taken alone and "sold" with anti-crime rhetoric are a cruel fraud on the public. Only restoring strong, no nonsense punishments for violent and chronic offenders will do that.

Sadly, the juvenile justice system is a blunt instrument. It only restores order through force. Yet, we must recognize that our first duty is to restore wholeness to those who are victims of violent crime. At a minimum we have an obligation to levy swift, sure justice to those who perpetrate heinous actions on the law-abiding. Until we can, with reasonable assurance, provide this, the right any of us have to walk the streets of this country without fear as our most constant companion is subject only to the conscience of a stray bullet.

REFORMS

On the subject of specific juvenile justice reforms, the NRA supports measures which are targeted directly at the juvenile offender and measures which establish reasonable uniform statewide regulation of minors carrying firearms. But, at the same time, these measures must also protect the rights of law-abiding minors, and their parents or guardians.

This year, in Arizona, the NRA helped draft legislation that would:

• Mandate holding a 16 or 17-year old juvenile offender responsible as an adult if the offender engaged in felony conduct involving the use or threatening exhibition of a deadly weapon or dangerous instrument, the intentional or knowing infliction of serious physical injury, or a sexual offense, unless the juvenile's participation was as an accomplice and was minimal;

• Mandate holding a 16 or 17-year old juvenile offender responsible as an adult if the offender on four prior and separate occasions had been adjudicated delinquent or if the offender had previously been committed to a juvenile correctional facility, unless the prior offenses were minor;

• Impose a felony penalty on parents or guardians who recklessly give consent to a minor to possess or carry a firearm;

• Encourage every school to provide a firearms safety program available at the option of the student's parent or guardian like NRA's "Eddie Eagle" program.

The NRA also supports legislation patterned after an Arizona law sponsored by State Representative Brenda Burns and passed by the Arizona Legislature which imposes severe mandatory felony penalties on adults who involve minors in criminal street gangs or drug trafficking.

CLOSING PUBLIC HOUSING TO CRIME ENTERPRISE

In some regions of the country, authorities are pressing to evict those in public subsidized housing who are using their residences as drug and gang centers. Charleston, South Carolina, Police Chief Rueben Greenberg instituted such a program. His critics charged he would have to evict 4,000 residents–literally half the Charleston public housing population. But Chief Greenberg writes, "We didn't have to evict nearly as many people as originally thought–only about 80 individuals." Why? Because they stopped engaging in criminal activity. Our catch-and-release justice system hobbles law enforcement. Says Chief Greenberg, "Whereas arrest had not prevented them from committing crimes...not having a place to sleep or live had a tremendous impact."

CAREER CRIMINALS

The statistics are alarming: one murder every 22 minutes, one forcible rape every 5 minutes, one violent crime every 22 seconds, one aggravated assault every 28 seconds. Every year nearly 5 million people in the U.S. are victims of violent crime. Most importantly, 7% of the criminals account for 80% of the violent crime. We must put a stop to this wave of violent crime by career criminals which is gripping our nation by passing comprehensive legislation that will reform the entire system from top to bottom. What is needed are laws that will take violent criminals off the streets, and keep them locked up, and laws that will restore swiftness and certainty of punishment to our criminal justice system.

Putting more police on the street is a necessary, but not sufficient, component in addressing violent crime. The only way to get the repeat, violent offenders off the street for good is to increase police presence and build more prisons to hold these career criminals. The amount of violent crimes has increased 531 percent since 1960, yet violent criminals are serving shorter sentences. The average time served by violent offenders is only 37% of the sentence given. Without a place to put those arrested, the state prison revolving door will simply spin faster. That is why H.R. 2872 proposes a cost-sharing agreement with the states to build a national system of regional prisons to house state violent criminals. To qualify for this partnership, states must require violent criminals to serve at least 85 percent of their sentences and enact mandatory minimum sentences for certain violent offenders. Unless comprehensive legislation is considered, this critical issue of prison overcrowding will not be addressed and deterrence and incapacitation of the truly dangerous will not be restored to the criminal justice system.

Excerpted from comments by Congressman Bill McCollum in a report by the House Judiciary Committee, November 9, 1993.

Because the "soldiers" in gang "armies" are so young, it pays to take out the "generals"–older gang kingpins who arm young people illegally and press them into crime. At the insistence of the community, joint police-prosecutor task forces can be formed to target older gang kingpins. After putting such a task force to work some years ago, one East Coast city reported a nearly 40 percent decrease in assaults, drive-by shootings and related youth gang activity.

WORST OFFENDERS

To identify the worst offenders, all customary agents of social control who intervene with youngsters–schools, courts, welfare agencies and police departments–must share information. Without information sharing, it is impossible to distinguish between those who might genuinely benefit from community outreach programs and those who are truly dangerous, repeat offenders.

The overwhelming majority of minors who use firearms do so responsibly and in a law-abiding manner under the supervision of parents or guardians. However, violent juvenile offenders must be subject to more certain punishment and that is why reform of our juvenile justice system is so urgently needed. The problem of youth violence is no more a lack of gun laws than it is an inadequate number of signs around school yards advising people that schools are weapons-free zones. The problem is a lack of moral muscle.

THE ENEMY

Speaking on the "Today Show" last year after a school shooting claimed the lives of two students, the principal of the school, Carol Burke-Beck, put it this way: "I am concerned that we are assuming as a society that all weapons are made out of metal. They are not. The enemy that we're trying to stop is the enemy of feeling hopeless, the enemy of being a victim, the enemy that I am someone who has to establish at every moment that I should be respected. We don't know how to love anymore and forgive anymore. Metal detectors do not detect that."

Not long ago, attitudes, pressures and sanctions once promoted a safe, healthy environment in schools. Not long ago, punishment was swift and sure, not slow and uncertain. The preservation of order in our society is directly related to a functioning, effective system of protection for the rights of Americans and prosecution of those who abuse those rights. Our democracy cannot survive without these protections. The NRA intends to do its part.

122

20   PREVENTING YOUTH VIOLENCE

THE FAILED "LOCK 'EM UP" POLICIES

Karabelle Pizzigati

Karabelle Pizzigati wrote the following article as Director of Public Policy for the Child Welfare League of America, a membership organization representing more than 700 public and voluntary child-serving agencies that assist over 2.5 million children and their families nationwide.

Points to Consider:

1. How is the social cost of violence portrayed?

2. What is the extent of youth violence?

3. Why has punishment failed as a strategy to prevent crime?

4. Identify the strategies that are explained to prevent crime.

Excerpted from testimony by Karabelle Pizzigati before the Subcommittee on Human Resources of the House Committee on Education and Labor, March 22, 1994.

One thing is certain–the "get tough, lock 'em up"
punitive approach, tried for years, has not worked.

Violent crime endangers every American family, and constitutes an immediate, pervasive threat to young people. The average age of homicide victims has grown younger and younger in recent years. Sixty-seven out of every 1,000 youth age 12 to 19 are victims of a violent crime each year, compared with 26 per 1,000 persons age 20 or older. Each day in the United States, 13 youths are killed by guns and at least 30 children are injured by guns. Since 1986, the number of children under age 18 killed in handgun homicides increased by 143 percent (compared with 30 percent for adults), from 602 in 1986 to 1,468 in 1992. Homicide is now the second leading cause of death among persons 15 to 24 years of age.

Though still too often viewed as an urban problem, violence endangers youth in suburban and higher-income neighborhoods. Even schools provide no safe haven. Each day, children carry an estimated 270,000 guns to school and every hour, 2,000 students are physically attacked on school grounds. Nearly one in four students and one in ten teachers say they have been victims of violence on or near school property.

The cost of violence is immense. Nationally, total health care costs because of criminal violence have been estimated to be more than $3.5 billion, with $1.5 billion resulting from firearms. The average cost to treat a child wounded by gunfire is more than $14,000. Hospital trauma centers, schools, and law enforcement agencies note disturbing trends in the seriousness of violent acts, availability of weapons, and youthfulness of victims, survivors, and aggressors.

Children in the child welfare system are particularly at risk of violence–many have already experienced abuse and are at greater risk of violence due to poverty, poor housing, lack of educational opportunity, alcohol and other drug abuse, and hopelessness. Young people who are victims of violence tend to be at greater risk than their peers of engaging in abusive, criminal, and delinquent behavior that victimizes others and of perpetrating violence themselves. The result can be a destructive cycle of violence that breeds child delinquents and adult criminals for generations to come.

124

Cartoon by Bob Gorrell. Reprinted with permission of **Coply News Service**.

MORE FAILURE

Our nation is frustrated by increased violent crime, overcrowded prisons, rising tax bills to pay for judicial, penitentiary, and personal security costs, and yet another generation of criminals made worse, not rehabilitated, by confinement. If we are unanimous that crime must be reduced, what should we do?

One thing is certain–the "get tough, lock 'em up" punitive approach, tried for years, has not worked. One important reason for its failure is that most serious crime is committed by young males in the 15-24 age group. The peak age for robbery and burglary is 17, and for aggravated assault, 21. Two-thirds of persons arrested for violent crime are under age 30. Therefore, our justice system, so committed to administering long prison terms, does two things wrong–first, it imprisons offenders for many years who might be more appropriately sentenced to shorter terms until they "age out" of criminal activity. Second, the justice system ignores crucial opportunities to prevent violence in the first place by not focusing violence prevention efforts on the very young. Attorney General Janet Reno has correctly stated the challenge– "If we wait for 16- and 17-year-olds to focus on delinquency prevention, it will be too late."

Given our nation's failure to solve the crime crisis, one would hope that Congress will take a new approach. Yet the bulk of the "get tough" Senate-passed crime bill (H.R. 3355) is hardly innovative. This legislation combines major Democratic and Republican initiatives into a huge $22.3 billion package of punitive and preventive anti-crime measures. It would throw money at tired and ineffective approaches such as building more prisons and tougher sentencing and new, unproven ideas like boot camps for youthful offenders. The bill institutes "three strikes and you're out" life imprisonment for third-time felons, sets minimum mandatory sentences for crimes involving guns, expands the death penalty to an additional 50 federal crimes, and places new limits on death row appeals.

If Congress approves legislation that, like the Senate bill, focuses overwhelmingly on punishment, it would be a costly mistake. Enactment of the "three strikes" proposal, for example, would require huge expenditures for new prison complexes to incarcerate thousands of eventually geriatric prisoners, a wasteful and expensive taxpayer venture. Community-based youth programs that prevent first-time and recidivist crime are far sounder investments.

Passage of the Senate bill would be costly, and not only because so much of the money would be wasted on ineffective anti-crime approaches. In addition to creating a $22.68 billion trust fund to pay its way, the bill lowers domestic discretionary caps by substantial amounts for the next five years, which could result in severe cuts in human services programs serving children.

PREVENTION IS A KEY COMPONENT OF ANTI-CRIME SUCCESS

Congress, the President, and the States must act to reverse rising violence, but they must balance punishment with prevention efforts which protect Americans from criminals today and prevent future crime by helping young people avoid becoming victims and victimizers. These strategies should feature significant support for activities that nurture and support at-risk youth with positive life opportunities. Helping at-risk youth avoid crime will produce greater dividends and cost savings than continuing to foot enormous hospital bills and after-the-fact punitive "solutions."

Crime prevention must be a central element in anti-crime efforts. Crime prevention encompasses many different strategies which assist at-risk youth or young people in general, young people exiting the juvenile justice system, young children, families,

126

CULTURE OF VIOLENCE

There are limits to how much violence you can reverse in a few days, because violence in society has been around for nearly 10,000 years. But there are not many societies where it has been so institutionalized as it has been in America. There are not many where it has been merchandised so creatively and ruthlessly by show business and weaponmakers. There has been no other society as huge and competitive, as restless and bountiful and as racially explosive as America. There is no other on that scale where some of the laws, on weapons, for example, so unabashedly invite violence.

Jim Klobuchar, "Children to Face Dark Questions on Culture of Violence," **Star Tribune**, October 11, 1992.

communities, or other groups of citizens. Prevention also includes some forms of intervention and rehabilitation that help prevent young people from becoming repeat offenders.

Public policy efforts should be directed toward improving intervention and rehabilitation of young people in the juvenile justice system. Since only a small percentage of young people commit most juvenile offenses, success in helping these young people improve their lives will contribute greatly toward preventing future juvenile and adult crime.

Unlike boot camps, which have little evaluation data, effective community-based programs for juvenile offenders have been studied and reveal that young people involved with the juvenile justice system benefit from diverse community-based services. A range of community-based intervention programs have been found to be successful in helping juvenile offenders avoid becoming repeat offenders. An Alabama juvenile work restitution program that matches juvenile offenders to appropriate public and private sector jobs has helped reduce recidivism by 10 percent since 1987. A study of community-based residential treatment for violent Utah youth found that only six percent of released offenders were charged with violent crimes within a year after release, and that most of the crimes were property-oriented.

Intervention services should include intensive case management, educational and employment assistance, counseling, and expanded use of family preservation. Helping young people

127

already in trouble avoid becoming career criminals is a crucial aspect of crime prevention.

Family preservation efforts provide a critical juvenile justice intervention approach. Comprehensive family preservation and support interventions have begun to show impressive results. A recent study found that multisystemic family preservation intervention to prevent recidivism and institutionalization of serious juvenile offenders was more effective at reducing long-term rates of criminal behavior and significantly less expensive than incarceration and usual service referrals.

CONCLUSION

Juvenile and adult violent crime can be reduced by investing in strategies that successfully address the root causes of crime and provide opportunities for young people. Instead of simply incarcerating and executing children, Congress must prevent crime by providing children with both productive alternatives to criminal activity and the skills and resources to lead a successful, non-violent existence. The serious problems our nation faces are all related—if we fail to keep our children from becoming victims and offenders, we will see further increases in crime, unemployment, welfare, health care costs, and family breakdowns. Congress must reject the foolish frenzy of "get tough" legislation and take sensible steps to reduce crime.

21   PREVENTING YOUTH VIOLENCE

TREAT YOUNG OFFENDERS
AS ADULTS

Richard M. Romley

Richard M. Romley wrote the following article as chief prosecutor for Maricopa County, the largest metropolitan district in Arizona (the Phoenix area).

Points to Consider:

1. What is wrong with rehabilitation efforts for young offenders?

2. How can rehabilitation efforts be effectively used?

3. What does sound public policy for young offenders demand?

4. Why should some young offenders be treated as adults?

Excerpted from testimony by Richard M. Romley before the Subcommittee on Juvenile Justice of the Senate Committee on the Judiciary, June 1 and 2, 1993.

He should be transferred and suffer the consequences of adult criminal sanctions.

The rise in violence in Maricopa County is well documented. Aggravating the issue of violence is the increased presence of gangs in Maricopa County. The Arizona Department of Public Safety estimates that there are approximately 783 gangs statewide with about 9,000 members.

The principle claim of the Juvenile Justice System...that, given enough resources (money) and enough time, they can "cure" (rehabilitate) anyone, or at least almost anyone, is neither realistic nor achievable. This attitude causes the Juvenile Justice System to always try program after program and, despite the expenditure of slightly over 8.7 million dollars for treatment in Maricopa County, the Juvenile Court asks for a blank checkbook to create more programs rather than facing up to the real issue. They should decide who truly belongs in the system.

LIMITED RESOURCES

Experience has shown that the Maricopa County Juvenile Court and the Department of Youth Treatment and Rehabilitation continue to expend the vast majority of their limited resources on the older juveniles who are either the most chronic or the most violent. These are the juveniles who are least likely to be amenable to treatment.

This has caused the public to lose confidence in the system and victims do not feel protected. Like the juveniles themselves, they feel the system is a joke and, given the recent rise in violence being committed by juveniles, the taxpayers are outraged. It is common knowledge that serious juvenile offenders quickly learn to manipulate the system and commit offense after offense. When the patience of the judge runs out and a transfer is ordered, the juvenile is shocked to find out that something "significant" will finally happen to him. Further, unlimited treatment opportunities fail to provide any incentive for a juvenile to modify his behavior.

TREATMENT

It is for these reasons that I would like to emphasize support for the underlying philosophy of the Juvenile Justice System as well as the necessity for the treatment and rehabilitation of juvenile offenders. However, limiting the number of the "bites of the

Cartoon by Mike Ramirez. Reprinted with permission of **Coply News Service**.

apple" before criminal sanctions are imposed is not logically inconsistent with that philosophy. Establishing some finite number of times that the system allows a particular juvenile to commit a felony is paramount in providing for public safety. Certainly, there should be no tolerance when the juvenile uses a gun or commits a violent act against another person. Public safety demands that we must limit that risk to only those juveniles who are most amenable to the services of the juvenile justice system!

BEHAVIOR

Because we are not dealing with an exact science but with human behavior, you will not find a juvenile justice professional who will tell you that they can predict whether any particular juvenile delinquent will recidivate. At best, they can only tell you who is potentially "at risk" to commit additional crimes.

Not only can they not predict future criminal behavior, their ability to prescribe the appropriate treatment to prevent further criminal conduct is basically still in the "stone age." It is merely a matter of experimentation until something either works or the juvenile has turned eighteen and is no longer in the system. Yet the attitude prevails that every juvenile is entitled to try everything before he suffers criminal consequences for his criminal conduct.

Compounding this weakness is the fact that whether it is services being delivered by the Juvenile Court or the Department, no

131

one knows what works on what kind of delinquent kids. Despite the expenditures of millions of dollars, outcome analysis has not been required to empirically demonstrate that any type treatment works.

TAX DOLLARS

Effective evaluation of programs is not only necessary to justify their significant expenditures of public monies, but also to validate the very premise of the juvenile justice system–that treatment and rehabilitation can stop criminal behavior. If this cannot be demonstrated, the entire system should fall. In hard economic times, and even in good, taxpayers do not deserve this irresponsible use of their tax dollars. The system must spend the limited taxpayer dollars more wisely by being honest and admitting that due to this uncertainty in diagnosis, the only true barometer to tell whether a juvenile is either amenable to treatment or willing to accept treatment is that juvenile's own conduct.

However well intended it may be to try to continue to find "the cure," the public does not deserve to be continually placed at risk. Simply stated, how many felonies should a citizen be subjected to by a particular juvenile? We must also send a message to violent juvenile offenders who, at least by the age of sixteen, can easily comprehend that their conduct is not acceptable and will not be tolerated in a civilized society.

PUBLIC POLICY

Sound public policy demands that, after reasonable efforts to rehabilitate have been made, the conclusion be reached that the juvenile has forfeited his right to receive the services and benefits of the juvenile system. He should be transferred and suffer the consequences of adult criminal sanctions.

Therefore, the Juvenile Court and the Department of Youth Treatment and Rehabilitation must make a philosophical shift to "front end spending." This would restore public confidence in the Juvenile Justice System by allowing them to expend their limited resources only on those juveniles who they can truly affect. Additionally, this would provide juveniles a very strong incentive to participate in their recovery and modify their behavior. However, rather than honestly admitting that the system keeps the wrong kids and keeps them too long, the system chooses to cloak these inherent weaknesses.

ADULTS AND JUVENILES

It also ignores the reality that there rarely, if ever, is a difference in maturity between an eighteen year old and a person seventeen years, eleven months, thirty days, and twenty-three hours old. Yet, for convenience, one arbitrary hour can result in significant consequence in terms of criminal sanctions. If one hour results in inappropriate disparity, what about one day, one week, three months, one year, etc? Clearly, the same rationale applies equally to the upper end of the proposed spectrum. Why arbitrarily pick the age of twenty-one? What about the person who is twenty years and one hour old? The same analysis applies.

ADULT SYSTEM

Not only does the arbitrary age incorrectly assume that three years will give sufficient time for treatment to cure all cases which fall "within the current evil" created by the present system, it again ignores the need for flexibility to provide age appropriate treatment and sanctions regardless of an arbitrary and fixed age. This can be done more efficiently in the adult system. In fact, the adult system is not devoid of treatment programs. Arizona is probably the leader in the United States in terms of intermediate sanctions. Not only does probation exist, there is intensive probation, day reporting, day fines, and an array of sanctions through the Community Punishment Act. It is also interesting to note that the current Juvenile Justice System does not have sufficient age appropriate treatment and rehabilitation programs for people of this age category.

22   PREVENTING YOUTH VIOLENCE

KEEPING EVERY CHILD SAFE: A PUBLIC HEALTH APPROACH TO VIOLENCE

Deborah Prothrow-Stith

Deborah Prothrow-Stith, M.D., is the Assistant Dean for the office of Government and Communications Programs at Harvard University. She is also the director of violence programs at the Injury Control Center in the Harvard School of Public Health.

Points to Consider:

1. What is meant by the term "acquaintance violence?"

2. Why is violence a "public health" problem?

3. How are schools essential for preventing violence?

4. What can be done by schools to improve the education of black males?

5. Describe needed institutional changes.

Excerpted from testimony by Deborah Prothrow-Stith before the Subcommittee on Juvenile Justice of the Senate Committee on the Judiciary, November 26, 1991.

About 50% of victims and assailants know each other; 20% of victims and assailants are members of the same family.

I bring a special perspective to the subject of curbing violence, especially violence in our schools and the streets of our cities, because I am a doctor and previously, Massachusetts public health commissioner. Now, as an assistant dean and member of the faculty at the Harvard School of Public Health, I am very involved in helping people, particularly doctors, understand adolescent violence as a public health problem.

During my internship at the Boston City Hospital, I became frustrated with the common attitude that violence among young adults, mostly black males, was somehow inevitable. I strongly believe that this violence, most of it what I call "acquaintance violence," is preventable.

VIOLENCE PREVENTION

There is no better setting than the schools to implement a violence prevention strategy. As public health practitioners, we know that some of the social and cultural influences related to the risk of violent behavior are not easily changed. Poverty, racism, adolescent developmental issues and gender expectations, are not easily changed. It is the personal, behavioral and spontaneous characteristics of violence that raise the most concern and which, fortunately, offer opportunities for intervention. About 50% of victims and assailants know each other; 20% of victims and assailants are members of the same family. One-half of homicides are precipitated by an argument, compared to only 15 % occurring in the course of committing another crime.

Evidence is mounting that violence is a learned response to stress and conflict. Violence on television has also been associated with violent behavior in children and youth. There are public health strategies currently being developed which directly respond to these facts about violence among youth today. In this statement, I will describe aspects of one such strategy: violence prevention programs for our schools.

SAVING CHILDREN

First, it is important to understand that I am talking about saving our children, helping our children to survive in a turbulent world which condones violence. Schools are an essential setting for helping children learn how to get along together. Historically, schools and public health have been partners in many types of prevention programs designed to respond to disease epidemics and health problems: vaccinations for polio, diptheria, mumps and measles; health and vision testing, innoculations for tuberculosis and screening for scoliosis; and courses about fitness, nutrition and reproduction, exercise and physical education programs, and so forth.

I submit to you that violence is a public health problem of epidemic proportions which can be remediated in the schools. There are two things the schools must do: (1) help kids learn and (2) help kids learn how to manage anger and conflict. Indeed, helping kids learn is especially complicated for inner-city black children.

The fact is that learning is a vital form of violence prevention. I am author of the first violence prevention curriculum for schools. Extensive work with the curriculum has shown that kids have to be able to use words, instead of force, to settle their differences. English, math and science skills help kids to reason through stressful and difficult situations. If we can successfully promote learning among all kids, we can promote survival of our children.

BLACK CHILDREN

The academic failure of black males is well documented. One in 4 black males ages 20-29 is incarcerated, on probation or on parole. Drop-out rates of black youth, especially boys, hover between 37% and 80% in inner-city schools in Los Angeles, Detroit, Chicago and Boston. Research by education experts has shown that racism and what has been called by some, "antagonism," misshapes the early childhood education experience of many black children. The teenagers who make it through high school are discouraged from trying higher education. This is in stark contrast to the well established fact that all kids in the first grade, given reasonably healthy starts, are hungry to learn. There are several aspects of this difficult phenomenon that can be turned around.

First, we must address teacher prejudice about the abilities of black children, i.e., expectations which are communicated to the child in the classroom. Studies of positive versus negative reinforcement show that the first predominates for white children,

WALKING TO SCHOOL

Eleanor Mill.

especially girls, and is particularly absent for little black boys. By the time these children have reached 10 or 11 years of age, the school and the children have frequently become adversaries.

Feelings of cynicism about their opportunities and personal potential supplant feelings of hopefulness and the desire to learn.

We know that what I call "high profile parenting" makes a difference for children. In a study which compared the school achievement of children by race, socioeconomic status and parent involvement, the achieving children had one thing in common–parents who cared and were able to be involved. The story of Jaime Escalante of Garfield High School, Los Angeles, featured in the movie "Stand and Deliver," exemplifies the gifted, inspired teacher. His special quality was teaching parents how to be involved in their children's education.

INSTITUTIONAL CHANGE

Institutional change must be fostered. Attitudes about children's potential have to change and expand. This country differs dramatically in its attitude toward learning from Israel and Japan, as two important examples. These cultures hold very dear the basic principle that all children can learn. In our system, the "tracking" of children starts early and, in a real sense, closes doors for most inner-city children. The failure feedback "loop," the cycle of discouragement that begins when a child ceases to be challenged and valued by his adult role models, has to be replaced by the success-building-upon-success experience which most white middle class children can take for granted.

This can occur when leadership within the schools requires such change. Dr. Jeff Howard's Efficacy Institute, based in Boston, works with school systems to improve academic achievement by challenging traditional assumptions about learning which "pigeonholes" children. He works with teachers and administrators to instill empathy for their less successful students and he works with children to re-shape their feelings about themselves. He points to the fact that children who can learn a spoken language at age three or four can fully develop their intelligence–but only with use. Self-confidence and serious effort, he says, are two critical ingredients for achievement which teachers can help to inspire in every child.

ANGER AND CONFLICT

The management of anger and conflict is the second major issue which schools can address. There is no better place to learn to assert one's own needs, opinions and angry feelings without los-

SUCCESSFUL PROGRAMS

There are examples of successful programs which have been included in the testimony before you. We must continue to create and expand such efforts to prevent violence. These strategies include successful primary and secondary prevention programs that work to:

- *change our social norms;*

- *redefine the characteristics of-heroes;*

- *promote and teach skills of getting along;*

- *promote and teach how to handle anger in powerful productive ways;*

- *teach parenting skills;*

- *encourage movies and television stories which portray successful non-violent problem solving.*

Excerpted from testimony by Deborah Prothrow-Stith before the House Select Committee on Children, Youth, and Families, March 10, 1993.

ing control than in the schools. Many have referred to this as the 4th "R"–relationships. The Peacemaker Program of New York City, a collaboration between the NYC Board of Education and Educators for Social Responsibility, provides a useful model for a program for children focused on building interpersonal and mediation skills.

The glamorizing of violence in the media compounds the problems of kids who don't learn about peaceful resolution of conflict at home, and makes programs like this one essential. The violence prevention curriculum for adolescents is designed to engage children, help them think about their own behavior, appreciate the control they can exert over their own behavior, and helps them to question their assumptions about the inevitability of fighting.

The curriculum helps kids look at the dynamics of fights, e.g., that fights always have a history and usually occur among acquaintances, and we role-play ways to resolve disputes and tense encounters. The embarrassment and loss of social standing in declining to fight, kids learn, will always be felt. But the higher cost of losing one's life or serious injury begins to gain importance for these children whose self-esteem is already low. Kids are taught that using anger constructively can change their world, rather than result in harm to themselves or peers.

CONCLUSION

It is important to recognize that kids who are asked to choose not to fight are beginning a new trend. This is difficult for most children. We live in a society which condones violence; television and movies frequently portray a hero who fights with guns and who never dies. What is the prescription for change? We must implement, throughout this society, violence prevention programs which change children's and parents' attitudes about violence, promote non-violence, and teach peaceful resolution of conflict.

23   PREVENTING YOUTH VIOLENCE

SAVE OUR CHILDREN FROM MEDIA VIOLENCE

Marion G. Etzwiler

Marion G. Etzwiler wrote this article as president of the Minneapolis Foundation, a non-profit organization that provides funding for groups that work with poverty and children's issues.

Points to Consider:

1. How do the media promote violence?

2. Why have children become big business in the media market place?

3. Why are boys especially susceptible to the world of violent entertainment?

4. Describe the six-point plan to counter the influence of television violence on children.

Marion G. Etzwiler, "Save Our Children from Infestation of Media Violence," **Star Tribune**, December 2, 1993. Reprinted with permission from **Star Tribune**, Minneapolis.

By age 18, an average American youth has witnessed about 26,000 television murders.

U.S. Attorney General Janet Reno's recent warning to TV producers should be applauded, if only for its symbolic value. It signals long-overdue recognition that violence prevention is going to require fundamental changes in the way our society cares for and protects children. That may mean regulating their exposure to violence the way we now regulate their exposure to pornography.

As influential as television is in the lives of our children and youth, it represents only one piece of a multibillion dollar entertainment industry that has helped create the culture of violence enveloping today's youngsters. Even for adults who are concerned about the problem, it is difficult to comprehend the omnipresence of media violence that shapes our children's values and behaviors.

To really understand, you would have to do more than watch children's weekend television programming, which features 15.5 violent acts per hour and is littered with commercials for violent games and toys. You would also have to sit through excruciating slasher films, ruthless "action hero" movies, and movies about turtle warriors who resolve every dispute with aggression. You would have to stand for hours at the video arcade playing games that depict a simplistic world of "them vs. us" and offer reward to those who torture, maim and murder enemies. You would have to listen to rap and heavy metal lyrics celebrating sadism, bigotry, homophobia and the violent subjugation of women. You would have to roam toy store aisles, examining the arsenal of pretend weapons, wrestling and military dolls, combat vehicles and he-man accessories that give children every opportunity to learn that violence is fun.

SOCIALIZING FORCE

Over the past few decades, children suffering the consequences of splintered families and working mothers have helped fill their empty hours with a new world of entertainment technologies, from Walkmans to cable TV. Chief among these is television, often referred to as the great American baby sitter. Without realizing it, many parents have virtually turned over the socialization of their children to the entertainment industry–a "teacher" motivated by profit margins rather than the best interests of impressionable

142

Cartoon by Mike Peters. Reprinted with permission of **Tribune Media Services**.

youth. Children have become big business in the media market-place, and the goal is to stimulate their spending, not to teach them responsible, pro-social values.

While entertainment media certainly are not the only socializing force acting upon our children, they have enormous authority in determining how youngsters see the world and pattern their own behavior. With such high levels of violence in television, films, video games, and certain kinds of lyrics, it is easy to see how children can fall victim to the "mean world" syndrome, viewing the world as a place where no one can be trusted and where the only means to resolve conflict is force.

BOYS

Boys especially are susceptible to the world of violent entertainment, where male heroes are defined by their power to destroy. Most vulnerable to identification with this kind of male brutality is the ever-increasing population of boys who grow up in fatherless homes, where no real-life male role models exist to offset distorted media images. In light of hundreds of studies that have concluded the viewing of violence leads to violent behavior, and the fact that nearly 90 percent of violent crimes in this country are committed by males, the proliferation of violent male role models in the entertainment industry is a clear and present danger.

The damaging, long-term impact media violence has on our children—and ultimately, on our communities—has led Dr. Myriam Miedzian, the author of *Boys Will Be Boys: Breaking the Link Between Masculinity and Violence*, to become one of the nation's leading advocates for stricter regulation of our children's exposure to such violence.

SIX-POINT PLAN

She has outlined a six-point plan for change that some might call radical. Yet with violence at the top of the domestic agenda and 80 percent of Americans convinced that there is too much violence on TV, the time has come to seriously consider bold new strategies. Miedzian's recommendations are:

- Undertake a nationwide public education campaign that makes adults aware of how influential entertainment media are in forming children's beliefs and attitudes.

- Create a National Children's Broadcasting system that sponsors non-commerical, pro-social programming for children on two channels, one for young children and one for teens.

- Develop a mandatory national rating system for films, videos and musical lyrics based on violent content.

- Require lockboxes on all new TV sets, allowing parents to prevent access by children to certain channels or to the TV itself.

- Pass federal legislation protecting children against violence in entertainment (similar to child labor and liquor prohibition laws).

- Pass state laws penalizing theater owners who allow children to be present at screenings of films adult-rated for violence or store owners who rent children adult-rated videos.

MINNESOTA

Miedzian, who has visited Minnesota several times in the past few years, recently made an observation about this state's potential for leadership on this issue that serves as a call to action for each of us. "From what I've seen," she said, "Minnesota is clearly ahead of other states in understanding and addressing the challenges of violence prevention. It's remarkable because your violence rates aren't particularly high compared to national averages, but your concern and determination outstrip what's happening even in places where crime is a huge problem. If a grassroots national initiative against media violence is going to begin anywhere, I would expect it to begin here."

My personal hope is that her expectations are well-founded and that this community will mobilize to create a humanistic, non-violent culture worthy of our children's trust.

24 PREVENTING YOUTH VIOLENCE

CENSORSHIP WON'T ELIMINATE VIOLENT CRIME

Stephen Chapman

Stephen Chapman is a nationally syndicated columnist. He wrote the following article for Creators Syndicate.

Points to Consider:

1. What assumptions are made about the relationship between media violence and social violence?

2. Has television become more violent or less violent?

3. How have politicians reacted to television violence?

4. Why is censorship of television violence a bad idea?

Stephen Chapman, "Censorship Won't Eliminate Violent Crime," **Human Events**, October 16, 1993. By permission of Stephen Chapman and **Creators Syndicate**.

A lot of countries have imported our TV series; few of them our crime rate.

The existence of a problem does not mean there is a solution. But politicians are not given to stoic acceptance of social imperfections, which they believe can be overcome by robust applications of government power. Congress is considering several measures to curb violence on television, an annoyance that has been inflated into a crisis so that politicians can let their consciences be our guide.

THE VIOLENCE

The assumption behind the proposals circulating on Capitol Hill is almost universally accepted: A society cannot subsist on an endless diet of televised violence without becoming unbearably violent itself. Kids who spend hours watching people do physical harm to one another, the theory goes, will grow up to do likewise. TV is violent: our society is violent and has grown more so since the rise of TV; therefore, it must be TV that makes us violent.

But we know that a society can be soaked in glamorized gore and be as placid as the prairies. Consider Canada, most of which has daily access to our programs and which remains stolidly resistant to the charms of violence. The United States has nine times as many people as Canada but 36 times as many homicides. A lot of countries have imported our TV series; few of them our crime rate. Nor does American lawlessness have any obvious connection to what goes out over the airwaves. The 1980s were only slightly more murderous than the 1930s, before TV could be blamed. The national habit of violence is not a recent creation of Steven Bochco.

LESS VIOLENCE

No one seems to have noticed that broadcast television has gotten less bloody in recent years, not more. Jack Valenti, head of the Motion Picture Association of America, said, "The 25 most popular series, most of which are situation comedies, have no violence." Police dramas, which used to be common, are now rare. Those who hoped to see a pacifying effect from this trend, though, have been disappointed.

Violence on TV may be no more to blame for crime in the streets than Judy Blume is for teen-age pregnancies—even a well-

147

Cartoon by Joe Heller.

known critic like University of Washington epidemiologist Brandon Centerwall estimates that watching TV makes kids only 5% more aggressive. But politicians hate to miss any chance to appease popular discontent.

POLITICAL ACTION

"I can tell you that none of the sponsors of these initiatives is losing votes back home with these ideas," acknowledges Illinois Sen. Paul Simon (D.). In the tradition of those Oklahomans who, it was said, would regularly stagger to the polls to vote dry, the public dislikes TV violence so much it can barely stand to keep the set on. There are several ideas percolating on Capitol Hill. Simon has asked the industry to take remedial action, while thoughtfully advising that if it doesn't, Congress will. The threat was enough to persuade the networks to start running parental advisories on graphic shows.

Rep. Edward Markey, the Massachusetts Democrat who chairs the telecommunications subcommittee, has proposed requiring TV makers to install a chip that would let owners block any show carrying a code signaling violent content. Sen. Ernest Hollings, South Carolina Democrat, wants to ban excessive violence except during the hours when most kids are in bed. Rep. John Bryant, Texas Democrat, suggests that the Federal Communications Commission deny license renewals to stations that offend congres-

148

┌───┐
│ ## TELEVISION PROGRAMS   │
│   │
│ *Make an effort to watch television for a week. Take notes* │
│ *while you do. Write to television stations and advertisers that* │
│ *sponsor violent programs and let them know you object to* │
│ *what you see. Take the time to let them know what kind of* │
│ *programming you like and want to see more of, too.* │
│   │
│ Sheila M. Miller, "To Turn Off Violence," **Star Tribune**, May 30, 1992. │
└───┘

sional standards.

GOOD VS. BAD VIOLENCE

But how do we separate good violence from bad violence? Presumably no one wants to regulate the content of local TV newscasts, some of which have made their living on the motto, "If it bleeds, it leads." Nor is anyone brave enough to suggest that the NFL or professional boxing be exiled to the middle of the night. And when PBS shows King Lear gouging out his own eyes or Henry V piling up French corpses at Agincourt, the TV police will probably not object. Brutality is fine if it's newsworthy, athletic or highbrow.

Congress may be able to find ways to alter the composition of broadcast TV without running afoul of the 1st Amendment, though it isn't easy. But the most gruesome fare is on cable and video, where the Supreme Court is no more likely to tolerate federal interference with content than it would in books and movies. So the value of forcing the networks to minimize mayhem is likely to be somewhere between tiny and zero.

That inconvenient fact aside, it would be a mistake to let the government expand its role in deciding what Americans should be allowed to see and hear of their own free will. Maybe some TV researcher could put aside the question of whether TV induces us to commit violence and investigate whether it causes us to demand that the government run our lives.

25   PREVENTING YOUTH VIOLENCE

SCRAPPING THE JUVENILE SYSTEM:
The Point

Gary B. Melton

Gary B. Melton, Ph.D., wrote the following article as the director of the Consortium on Children, Families, and the Law at the University of Nebraska.

Points to Consider:

1. How are juveniles treated in the justice system?

2. Why should the present juvenile court system be scrapped for a new one?

3. Should there be a separate juvenile court system? Is it separate now?

4. Define the UN Convention on the Rights of the Child.

5. Explain the author's new plan for changing the juvenile justice system.

Excerpted from testimony by Gary B. Melton before the Subcommittee on Juvenile Justice of the Senate Committee on the Judiciary, March 4, 1992.

I do believe that a separate juvenile court is desirable.

Just 25 years ago the Supreme Court described juvenile courts as "kangaroo courts." That label is too harsh for the situation today. Nonetheless, it is fair to say that many juvenile courts still do not seriously apply the Supreme Court's proclamation that the Bill of Rights does not belong to adults alone. Nonexistent or inadequate legal representation for juvenile respondents is a gross example of many juvenile courts' failure to protect the rights of children before them. Moreover, the historic rationales for a separate juvenile court system have failed to withstand empirical scrutiny.

I do believe that a separate juvenile court is desirable, but it should be a new court that has more procedural protections than adult criminal court–not fewer, as has been the tradition in the juvenile court since its inception a century ago. I also believe that the juvenile court should be just one part of a comprehensive system for advocacy and protection of children's interests. Moreover, the federal government has an important role and responsibility to ensure that children's rights under the Constitution and federal statutes are taken seriously by state and federal authorities and that effective means are available for monitoring and advocacy on behalf of children.

CHILDREN'S RIGHTS

The UN Convention on the Rights of the Child provides a useful guide to the rudiments of due process for juveniles. Besides enumerating specific procedural rights that are guaranteed by the U.S. Constitution, such as the right to counsel and the privilege against self-incrimination, the Convention requires that juvenile delinquents be treated "in a manner consistent with the child's sense of dignity and worth, which reinforces the child's respect for the human rights and fundamental freedoms of others." Shamefully, the United States stands virtually alone among developed nations in its failure to sign or ratify the UN Convention.

Psychological research shows that satisfaction with the legal process is affected by the degree of control respondents have in the presentation of their cases and the courtesy with which they are treated by legal authorities. Research shows further that juveniles rarely are skilled in exercising their rights (even when they have previous involvement in the legal system), that parents of juvenile respondents rarely are effective advocates for their chil-

Cartoon by Joe Sharpnack.

dren in the juvenile court, and that, absent extraordinary efforts, juveniles often do not regard their rights as irrevocable entitlements.

LEGAL RIGHTS

In short, due process is different for juveniles. Although protection of liberty and privacy is profound for juveniles as well as adults, procedures should be especially rigorous if juvenile respondents are to make good use of the legal system. Special efforts also are necessary if juveniles are to believe that they are being treated fairly and that they truly have a say.

Of course, the need for advocacy does not end with adjudication. Class action suits have provided vivid evidence of the overuse of institutional placement, the atrocious conditions of confinement in some training schools, detention centers, and private treatment facilities, and the lack of sufficient effective, individualized treatment alternatives in most jurisdictions.

Similarly, the need for advocacy is not limited to youth in the juvenile justice system. Adequate legal representation may be an even greater issue in other contexts (e.g., child protection; divorce) in which children become involved with the legal system. Moreover, as a matter of both ethics and socialization into democratic ideals–arguably the primary purpose of public education–children should be given the opportunity to express their opinions and describe their experiences relevant to issues affecting them in public policy and practice.

Family advocacy also should be given greater attention. Recent research evidence shows that, for perhaps the first time in American history, parents often do not believe that they can count on their neighbors to assist them with problems involving the parents' children. Therefore, the need is also clear for advocates to assist parents in maneuvering the complex service system on behalf of their families.

NEW PLAN

With these points in mind, I respectfully recommend the following amendments to the Juvenile Justice and Delinquency Prevention Act:

• *Congress should establish a new Office on Child Advocacy in the Department of Justice and authorize $10 million for discretionary grants to be administered by it.*

That Office should have responsibility for research and demonstration projects and related training and dissemination activities designed to develop and improve advocacy for children, both within and outside the juvenile justice system. For example, the Office should support research and training designed to assist lawyers and other advocates in their representation of children. It also should conduct research and training aimed at the development of legal structures and procedures that, consistent with the UN Convention on the Rights of the Child, promote children's sense of dignity and worth. The Office also should stimulate opportunities for self-advocacy by children and other activities that promote children's appreciation of democratic values.

• *Congress should establish a program of incentive grants to States for development of offices of ombudsmen for children. Twenty-five million dollars should be authorized for the program.*

Having carefully studied the office of the Ombudsman for Children in Norway and also being familiar with similar offices in other jurisdictions with cultures similar to our own (e.g., Israel; New Zealand; South Australia), I am amazed by the speed with which such offices become identified and accepted by both children and adults as spokespersons for children's interests. A network of independent, accessible state ombudsmen for children would go far toward ensuring a place for children in American law and politics, preventing their neglect by state and federal authorities, and promoting children's appreciation of democratic values.

• *Congress should condition States' receipt of formula grants for juvenile justice on their provision of counsel for all juveniles accused of delinquent or status offenses.*

Nearly two decades ago, the Supreme Court acknowledged that "it is simply too late in the day to conclude...that a juvenile is not put in jeopardy at a proceeding whose object is to determine whether he has committed acts that violate a criminal law and whose potential consequences include both the stigma inherent in such a determination and the deprivation of liberty for many years." That many juveniles still are subjected to such jeopardy without representation by counsel is a travesty of justice.

CONCLUSION

Congress should condition receipt of federal funds on a state's guarantee of a right to counsel that is unwaivable by or on behalf of juveniles except under extraordinary circumstances, because such a right is so clearly fundamental in an adversary system. As I have noted, though, such a "string" is insufficient by itself to guarantee meaningful representation of children's interests. To ensure that federal rights are fulfilled requires that the federal government launch an initiative to develop a knowledge base that will enable

154

attorneys and other advocates to represent children in a way that their voices will be heard and that they will feel that they have a say in matters affecting them. Such an approach is morally imperative, because we respect our youngest citizens as persons and therefore owe them due process of law. It is politically imperative, because we want to promote and sustain a democratic legal system in which citizens are participants, not objects.

26 PREVENTING YOUTH VIOLENCE

SCRAPPING THE JUVENILE SYSTEM:
The Counterpoint

David B. Mitchell

David B. Mitchell wrote this article as the judge of the Circuit Court for Baltimore, Maryland.

Points to Consider:

1. How is the juvenile court system described?

2. Why should the current system not be scrapped for a new one?

3. How well are the rights of those who appear before the juvenile courts protected?

4. What are the strengths of the current system?

5. What are the weaknesses?

Excerpted from testimony by David B. Mitchell before the Subcommittee on Juvenile Justice of the Senate Committee on the Judiciary, March 4, 1992.

I am puzzled by those who argue that the system should be scrapped.

The basic structure of the juvenile court in Baltimore City was determined in the era of World War II. There would be one member of the Circuit Court Bench designated to preside in juvenile matters. An official appointed by the Bench was designated to assist the juvenile court judge in the fact finding aspects of its duties and make recommendations as to appropriate dispositions of the cases so referred.

JUVENILE COURT

The juvenile court has not been given either the attention or resources to remain current with the issues it was called upon to confront. As a consequence, it has not remained current with the problems of the moment. It literally functions in a pen and quill environment in the era of rapid telecommunications. This is due mainly to a lack of leadership in the judiciary for these problems going back decades and the indifference of the political community to the structural needs of the court.

To this must be added the demands placed on the criminal justice system. It has become "the horse that eats all the oats in the barn." The need for more and more prison space, and more and more police to enforce the laws, and more and more judges and prosecutors to protect the public from the acts of the adult populations has driven the system. The juvenile justice system has been left to fend for itself. The concentration of those who make the policy decisions and allocate the funds to wage wars on crime and drugs have neglected the juvenile justice system in the process.

SCRAPPING THE SYSTEM

The net result is that the juvenile justice system has been left ill equipped to respond to the present challenges. That is one of the reasons I am puzzled by those who argue that the system should be scrapped. If not this, then they must be prepared to return "back to the future" of the pre-juvenile court era of a century ago. Then underage offenders were tried and incarcerated with the adult population without regard to their youth. If not that, then a new court system would have to be created. Scrapping the juvenile court is akin to throwing out the baby with the bath water. It needs the attention of the judiciary and political community to make it more effective than it has been. It requires this assistance to reach its potential. There are reforms that should be made as with any bureaucratic endeavor. That, however, in my view is not a justification to end the court.

POLITICS

Similarly, the support system of the juvenile court must have the consistent attention of the political community. The focus of that support system must be more toward prevention and early intervention and away from detention and incarceration. Numerous studies of the treatment alternatives for juveniles have demonstrated that effective community-based treatment is less costly and more effective than massive training schools. In Maryland it cost the taxpayers a average of $55,000 a year to incarcerate a juvenile offender in its only training school. Contrast that with the $12,000 annualized cost of many community-based non-residential treatment facilities. Not only does the cost ratio favor this form of treatment, but the recidivism rates do as well. This then should be emphasized in Maryland. Unfortunately, because my state is in the throes of a fiscal and economic crisis, all levels of government are downsizing. The Baltimore City court is left with the alternatives of an overworked probation staff and the training school. Both are already bursting at the seams.

RIGHTS

The rights of those who appear before the court, whether it is the accused, the victim or the parent, are of paramount importance to my court. I dare say every juvenile court judge or master with whom I have had contact over the past eight years of service as a judge has been concerned with the rights of those who appear before them. This must be particularly so in the juvenile court where children are at issue. To suggest otherwise concerns me. It also suggests to me that the reviewers have not attended a session of a court.

It has also been my privilege to serve as faculty at training sessions for juvenile court judges and masters, attorneys and case workers for the eight years of my judicial service. That has been both in Maryland and in other parts of America. I have lectured in Mississippi to juvenile judges and prosecutors and defenders on juvenile law and procedure. It has been my experience that these professionals are not prepared to permit any trammelling upon the

Cartoon by Gary Markstein.

rights of any participant without a vigorous challenge. The roads to the appellate court are well known to juvenile court participants.

LEGAL COUNSEL

Juveniles charged with committing acts that if done by an adult would be crimes are represented by attorneys throughout their appearances before the court. This is the case from the moment that child first appears in court until the case is closed. No action of the court ever occurs when the child is represented without the presence and knowledge of that attorney. Less than one half of one percent of children in delinquency cases is unrepresented by counsel. In Baltimore City, that counsel is provided by the state-funded Office of the Public Defender. Its Juvenile Court Division is excellent. Perhaps I am prejudiced to some extent, because I once served there myself. The due process and other rights of the accused are safeguarded vigorously!

The public, and the political community, do not understand the juvenile court system of justice. I dare say most judges do not know or understand it themselves. The proceedings are closed to the general public. There is the suspicion that what is done

SEATTLE AND VANCOUVER

Look at the assault rate. In Seattle and Vancouver, assaults by sticks and bats and fists are about the same [numbers]; also about the same are assaults by knives. However, the assault by guns is about four times greater in Seattle than in Vancouver. People ask the question, "Do guns kill people, or do people kill people?" This study suggests that, in fact, guns play a big role.

Deborah Prothrow-Stith, "Fighting Is a Lousy Way to Lose a Friend," **Christian Social Action**, June, 1993.

beyond a person's gaze is suspect. Quite naturally, those who do not know are suspicious. My own colleagues, most of who react with horror at the suggestion to serve in the juvenile court, did not comprehend the multitude of problems and challenges encountered in the juvenile court, until they read my report to the Russell Committee. Now they are supportive of change. Before they did not know, were not informed, or did not bother to be informed. The same is true with the political community. It was easier to rail against it than to learn it. One of the reasons I consented to writers and photographers from *Time* magazine spending a month in the Baltimore City court was to have the public see and understand what happens to families and children in court. We wanted the public to know that there are dedicated and hard working people there attempting to do the public's business.

NEW FOCUS

No juvenile court system is going to be effective unless and until a shift in focus occurs in the treatment of offenders. Earlier identification and concentration of resources is the key. Preventive measures must be brought to the fore. School truancy cannot go untreated. We do not get the cases until the child has missed something like 120 out of 180 days in the school year. The staff of the school system that is charged with preparing and presenting these cases was cut years ago as an effort to save money by our local school system. If a child misses two-thirds of a school year, it's too late to bring the matter to court. There is not much that we can do. Earlier intervention is necessary.

If you want to help the system, provide the funds to make it

160

work. If you want to help, spend some time (defined here as a month or more) of a concentrated nature in the juvenile courts of this nation's cities. I challenge you and your staffs to visit the successful community-based treatment models run by the public and private communities throughout America. I challenge you and your staffs to not let the naysayers rule the day. The juvenile courts of America are indeed "waging a thankless struggle to save society" lost children.

READING THE DAILY NEWSPAPER

This activity may be used as an individualized study guide for students in libraries and resource centers or as a discussion catalyst in small group and classroom discussions.

One of the best sources for obtaining current information on the state of American youth and adolescent violence is the daily newspaper. The skill to read with insight and understanding involves the ability to know where to look and how to "skim" the headlines for articles of interest. The best place to begin is the front section and the opinion/editorial pages. Other good sources include the sections on the economy and any special feature sections that are usually included in Sunday editions. Be sure not to overlook the sections that deal with local issues as they often contain stories of global concern that are happening in your own community.

Guidelines

Using newspapers from home or from your school or local library, skim the headlines and locate articles that deal with the broad issue of youth violence. Topics such as gangs and firearm violence are appropriate subjects to locate. With the alarming attention the issue of adolescent violence has gained, today's headlines and editorials are a good source of information on the issues brought out in this book.

1. Try to locate several articles dealing with the topics of this chapter.

2. Do any of the articles or opinions express alternatives to youth violence? If so, how do they agree or differ with the alterna-

tives expressed throughout the readings in Chapter Four?

3. Which alternatives in Chapter Four do you feel have shown positive results or have potential to foster resistance to violence? Use your selected articles to support your statement.

4. Do you feel that local, state and national governments are effectively dealing with the epidemic of youth violence? Why or why not? (Be sure to refer to your newspaper sources.)

5. Can you locate any articles or editorials that refute the content of any of the readings in this publication? If so, explain.

Other Projects

Start a scrapbook of articles, editorials and political cartoons concerning issues of adolescent violence. Prepare a short essay highlighting the impact of violence upon youth today. Be sure to record any local incidents of "closer to home" news along with research of the problem on the national level.

BIBLIOGRAPHY

Youth Violence

Anderson, E. "The code of the streets" [inner city black community and the code of respect], **Atlantic Monthly** v273 (May 1994): p80-3+.

Beardsley, T. "Desperate measure" [pros and cons of government research into violent behavior], **Scientific American** v271 (July 1994): p24.

Dunkel, T. "Newest danger zone: your office," **Working Woman** v19 (August 1994): p38-41+.

Gest, T. and D. R. Friedman. "The new crime wave" [teen violence], **U.S. News & World Report** v117 (August 29 - September 5, 1994): p26-8.

Hazlett, T. W. "Guns, drugs, and rock 'n' roll," **Reason** v25 (March 1994): p66.

Polsby, D.D. "The false promise of gun control" [cover story], **Atlantic Monthly** v273 (March 1994): p57-60+.

Simm, M. "Violence study hits a nerve in Germany" [criticism of work of H.H. Ropers], **Science** v264 (April 29, 1994): p653.

Stevens, J. "Treating violence as an epidemic" [cover story], **Technology Review** v97 (August/September 1994): p22-30.

Topolnicki, D. M. "Voices from the mean streets" [Baltimore children as victims], **Money** v23 (June 1994): p129-31+.

"The United States of violence" [cover story; special section], **USA Today** (Periodical) v122 (May 1994): p22-42+.

Updegrave, W. L. "You're safer than you think," **Money** v23 (June 1994): p114-17+.

"Violent incidents on the rise," **USA Today** (Periodical) v122 (April 1994): p5-6.

Media Violence

Appleyard, B. "Curbing a culture of violence," **World Press Review** v41 (March 1994): p24-5.

Federman, J. "What other countries do about ratings," **Media & Values** no63 (Fall 1993): p15.

Felde, K. "No more blood at eleven: TV news needs to report conflict responsibly," **Media & Values** no63 (Fall 1993): p12.

Fischer, R. L. "Is it possible to regulate television violence?" **USA Today** (Periodical) v123 (July 1994): p72-5.

Kurtz, S. "Voodoo and violence" [interview with P. Jillette], **Reason** v25 (April 1994): p35-9.

Lapham, L. H. "Burnt offerings," **Harper's** v288 (April 1994): p11-15.

Link, D. "Facts about fiction: in defense of TV violence" [cover story], **Reason** v25 (March 1994): p22-6.

"Media and violence: part two: searching for solutions" [cover story; special issue; with editorial comment by Elizabeth Thoman], **Media & Values** no63 (Fall 1993): p1-24.

"Prime-time violence: is it hurting your kids?" **Ladies' Home Journal** v111 (January 1994): p44.

Silver, R. "Media must tell truth about violence" [interview with D. Prothrow-Stith], **Media & Values** no63 (Fall 1993): p6.

Sragow, M. "The homeric power of Peckinpah's violence" [director's cut of The wild bunch to be rated NC-17], **Atlantic Monthly** v273 (June 1994): p116-18+.

Wilson, B. J. "What's wrong with the ratings?" **Media & Values** no63 (Fall 1993): p13-15.

Gangs

Block, Carolyn Rebecca and Richard. "Street gang crime in Chicago," **Washington, National Institute of Justice** (1993).

Bonney, Lesley Suzanne. "The prosecution of sophisticated urban street gangs: a proper application of RICO," **Catholic University Law Review** v42 (Spring 1993): p579-613.

Conkin, P. "Can you read the handwriting on the wall?" [Fr. G. Boyle's work with gang members at L.A.'s Dolores Mission Church], **U.S. Catholic** v57 (December 1992): p28-34.

Conly, Catherine H. "Street gangs: current knowledge and strategies," **Washington, National Institute of Justice** (1993).

DeMont, J. "A town in terror" [hoodlums in Moser River, N.S.], **Maclean's** v106 (November 8, 1993): p50+.

"Gang leaders begin new agenda: unity" [National Urban Peace and Justice Summit], **Jet** v84 (May 24, 1993): p5.

Ingrassia, M. "Life means nothing" [adolescent brutality], **Newsweek** v122 (July 19, 1993): p16-17.

Kantrowitz, B. "Wild in the streets" [teen violence; cover story], **Newsweek** v122 (August 2, 1993): p40-6.

"National Gang Summit draws leaders to Chicago," **Jet** v85 (November 8, 1993): p13.

Presser, A. L. "On the other side of the tracks" [Chicago conference], **National Review** v45 (November 29, 1993): p46.

"Role model" [L. Bing, expert on Los Angeles gangs], **The New Yorker** v69 (July 19, 1993): p25-6

Stacey, M. "Bad boys" [group sexual attacks on girls], **Seventeen** v52 (November 1993): p124-7+.

Youth & Firearms

Buckley, J. "The tragedy in room 108 [G. S. Pennington murders D. McDavid and M. Hicks at East Carter High in Grayson, Ky.], **U.S. News & World Report** v115 (November 8, 1993): p41-4+.

Diamond, E. "Guns and poses" [Harvard Project on Guns, Violence and Public Health enlists the aid of TV shows], **New York** v26 (December 6, 1993): p32+.

Glastris, K. "Live theater for the MTV crowd" [Gunplay], **U.S. News & World Report** v114 (May 10, 1993): p20.

Hull, J. D. "A boy and his gun" [cover story], **Time** v142 (August 2, 1993): p20-7.

Kantrowitz, B. "Wild in the streets" [teen violence; cover story], **Newsweek** v122 (August 2, 1993): p40-6.

Karlsberg, E. "I was shot!: a shooting victim's ordeal," **Teen** v38 (July 1994): p21-2+.

Karlsberg, E. "Young guns: tragic tales," **Teen** v37 (July 1993): p26+.

Larson, E. "The story of a gun" [cover story], **The Atlantic** v271 (January 1993): p48-52+.

"Reading, writing and murder" [special section], **People Weekly** v39 (June 14, 1993): p44-54.

Reynolds, R. "Kids who kill" [school violence; charts], **Black Enterprise** v23 (July 1993): p47.

Romer, R. "Guns in the hands of kids" [address, September 7, 1993], **Vital Speeches of the Day** v60 (November 1, 1993): p58-62.

Von Hoffman, N. "Gun crazy" [school violence], **The New Yorker** v69 (August 2, 1993): p23.

Juvenile Justice

Butts, Jeffrey A. and Howard N. Snyder. "Restitution and juvenile recidivism," **Bureau of Justice Statistics** (September 1992).

Carlson, M. B. "Order on the court" [criticism of the crime bill], **Time** v144 (August 29, 1994): p35.

Colapinto, J. "A boy and his gun" [E. Kalobius kills A. Grenier in Sicklerville, N.J.], **Rolling Stone** (October 6, 1994): p64-6+.

Collins, Jessica. "Trial by a jury of teen peers," **Insight (Washington Times)** v8 (June 21, 1992): p12-16, 30.

Couloumbis, Angela E. "'Boot Camps vs. Jail: the jury is still out," **Christian Science Monitor** (March 2, 1994): p1-3.

Gest, T. and D. R. Friedman. "The new crime wave" [teen violence], **U.S. News & World Report** v117 (August 29 - September 5, 1994): p26-8.

Gibbs, N. R. "Murder in miniature" [death of R. Sandifer; cover story], **Time** v144 (September 19, 1994): p54-9.

Ingrassia, M. "Learning to walk away," **Newsweek** v124 (August 15, 1994): p47-9.

"Judgment Day" [14 year old E. Smith convicted for murdering D. Robie in Savona, N.Y.], **People Weekly** v42 (August 29, 1994): p90.

"Juvenile Justice: should 13-year-olds who commit crimes with firearms be tried as adults?" **American Bar Association Journal** v80 (March 1994): p46-47.

"Kids who kill" [Canada; cover story; special section; with editorial comment by Carl Mollins], **Maclean's** v107 (August 15, 1994): p2, 32-9.

Lacayo, R. "When kids go bad," **Time** v144 (September 19, 1994): p60-3.

Miller, Zell. "Do boot camps work?" **Atlanta Journal and Constitution** (February 20, 1994): p1-2.

Pipho, C. "States get tough on juvenile crime," **Phi Delta Kappan** v75 (December 1993): p286-7.

"Reducing number of repeat offenders" [EQUIP program], **USA Today** (Periodical) v122 (April 1994): p6.

Riley, Michael. "Corridors of agony," **Time** v139 (January 27, 1992): p48-51, 54-55.

Roush, David W. "Juvenile detention programming," **Federal Probation** v57 (September 1993): p20-33.

Smith, C. S. "Kids' stuff" [weapons used by New York City youth], **New York** v27 (August 8, 1994): p34-7.

Smolowe, J. "Out of the line of fire" [cities campaign against teenage violence], **Time** v144 (July 25, 1994): p25.

Tapia, A. "Healing our mean streets" [Christians working to stem violent crime], **Christianity Today** v38 (July 18, 1994): p46-8.